AMERICAN ANTIQUE TOYS

1830~1900

AMERICAN ANTIQUE TOYS

1830~1900

Bernard Barenholtz / Inez McClintock
Photographs by Bill Holland

Harry N. Abrams, Inc., Publishers, New York

Page 2: **Humpty Dumpty or Clown Bank**

C. G. Shepard. Patented 1882. Cast iron, height 7½"

Page 3: Clockwise from top left:

Detail of Alphabet Man *(see page 36)*.

Detail of Santa in Sleigh with Goats *(see page 149)*.

Detail of Uncle Sam with Flag *(see page 67)*.

Detail of General Grant Smoking a Cigar *(see page 80)*.

Page 4: **Columbia Bell Toy**

Gong Bell. 1880s. Cast iron, length 9½"

Project Editor: Edith M. Pavese

Editor: Lory Frankel

Designer: Wei-Wen Chang

Library of Congress Cataloging in Publication Data

Barenholtz, Bernard.
    American antique toys 1830–1900.

    Includes index.
    1. Toys—United States—History—19th century.
2. Toys—United States—Collectors and collecting
—United States. I. McClintock, Inez Bertail,
joint author. II. Title.
GV1218.5.B37   745.592'0973   80-10841
ISBN 0-8109-0668-6

Library of Congress Catalogue Card Number: 80-10841

Printed and bound in Japan

CONTENTS

NOTES AND ACKNOWLEDGMENTS

This is a story about antique and collectible toys, some manufactured, some folk art toys, all created in America from 1830 to the turn of the century.

When I was first approached by the publisher to create this book my initial reaction was, do we really need yet another book about old toys? A number of books published more recently, such as David Pressland's *The Art of the Tin Toy,* Jac Remise and Jean Fondin's *The Golden Age of Toys,* Mary Hillier's *Automata and Mechanical Toys,* and earlier works by Karl Gröber, Katharine McClinton, Leslie Daiken, Henri d'Allemagne, Louis Hertz, and Marshall and Inez McClintock should be sufficient, I thought, to keep collectors well informed. After reviewing the literature about old and collectible toys it became apparent that there was a place for another but different kind of toy book. Most of the other works concerned themselves with European toys, having only an occasional reference or photograph of an American toy. The exceptions were Louis Hertz's *Handbook of Old American Toys* and Marshall and Inez McClintock's *Toys in America,* both out of print, plus a few other out-of-print titles. Most of these treated the subject by identifying the toy or manufacturer or giving a detailed history of the toy manufacturing industry in the United States, all very important contributions to collectors.

After several years and much urging from the publisher, I agreed to do this book, and decided to approach it in a slightly different way. As a co-founder of Creative Playthings, Inc., having done graduate studies in child development and early childhood education, I am interested in how children used their toys, in what nineteenth-century children were like, and in comparing the influences on the toy designers and toy manufacturers today to those of the period covered in this book. One of the ways for me to approach the subject was to analyze the toys based on the categories in which they were designed or produced. In sorting through hundreds of old toys in my collection I began to see the various categories that toys fell into. There are toys with eagle patterns, flags, and Uncle Sam figures, and toys designed around political and historical characters and events. It became obvious that some of the important themes of toy designers of the period were the "Symbols of Freedom." Other categories that designers used extensively were "Toys to Grow On," "Familiar Animals," "The Circus," "Strictly for Pleasure," which included toys of sports, recreation, and pleasure vehicles, "Race and Chase," "Fairy Tales and Fantasy," and toys reflecting "The Workaday World."

As I grouped the toys into these various categories I could not help but reflect on my Creative Playthings years. Surely the categories of toys that were popular in the 1800s were very much the same as those Creative Playthings marketed for children of the middle of the twentieth century. We designed and produced infant toys, building blocks, push and pull toys, transportation toys, play-people in the form of the family as well as community helpers—play-people dressed in a variety of work clothing designating the delivery man, the fireman, the railroad engineer, and others. Then there were familiar animals, very important accessories to be used with block building, and pleasure vehicles—a car for the entire family to drive out to the park or wherever the child's imagination took it. In each category I saw parallels between modern toys and those produced by the Francis, Field and Francis Company in 1840, or George W. Brown and Company in 1870, and all the other early American toy makers.

What is different about the toys of the mid-twentieth century from those of the nineteenth century? The only real differences are in the nature of the materials and the technology of the time, and in designs influenced by the directions of today's political, social, economic, and environmental conditions. The fireman of the 1800s on a horse-drawn fire engine performed the same job as today's fireman, the latter dressed slightly differently and riding a sleek motorized fire engine. Today's toy fire engines, like the real ones, are housed in a fire station, as the toy fire engines of the 1800s were housed in firehouses made by Crandall, Reed, Ives, and other companies. This is but a single example repeated hundreds of times when we compare what was yesterday with what is today in the world of toys. In addition to illustrating some old toys, many of which have not generally been shown elsewhere, I wanted to share some personal thoughts about collecting, some collecting experiences, and some thoughts about toys for fun and toys for learning in the nineteenth century.

Our interest here is not primarily concerned with who made what, although we have included information about early toy manufacturers where it was available. A great deal of information about American toys and their makers has surfaced in the past thirty years. Early toy manufacturers' catalogues have been found as well as molds, dies, cartons, boxes, bookkeeping ledgers, and other items, all of which has helped us as collectors to be better able to identify the old toys we cherish. However, this is still a meager amount of knowledge to help us identify many of these objects and the search for more information continues. Where we have been able to positively identify a maker we have listed the company. Where we have some doubts but have some educated guessing we call it an attribution. Where we don't have the slightest idea we have simply said "unknown."

We have deliberately excluded from this work certain categories and types of toys although they may have been very popular with the children of the 1800s. For example, we have not included dolls, dollhouses, and miniatures; trains other than trackless pull or clockwork types; automotive toys produced in the the late 1800s; and other types of toys to be found in general toy collections (although these are more often to be found in collections of specialized interest).

The toys included are mostly from my collection, with some examples from the

Holland Collection. As mentioned earlier, all of the toys illustrated were manufactured or carved in America from about 1830 to the turn of the century. They are usually referred to by collectors as antique toys, but the application of the term "antique" means at least one hundred years old. Some of the very desirable pieces included here might be only seventy-five or eighty years old, so we must consider them as old or collectible pieces.

In a book such as this good photography is very important. One of my specific requests of the publisher was that we have Bill Holland do the photography. Bill is not only well-known in his vocation as a professional photographer but is also a highly regarded collector of old toys and folk art. We have been collector friends for about twenty years so I knew that his creative and technical skills as a photographer were among the best in the field, and that his sensitivity in knowing how to present the toys in the context of their categories would be of interest to toy collectors, photographers, designers, or anyone interested in pleasurable viewing.

In addition to having Bill Holland associated with the book I felt that to be the best book of categories of early American toys we should have Inez McClintock join us as a collaborator. Inez has a great interest in American toys and is herself a collector.

Our special thanks to Blair Whitton, Curator of Toys at the Margaret Woodbury Strong Museum in Rochester, New York, for his help in documenting one of the earliest wooden toys manufactured in the United States. Thanks to Scudder Smith, publisher of *Antiques and the Arts Weekly,* who first printed some of my experiences as a collector, written in connection with the Barenholtz exhibit at the Abby Aldrich Rockefeller Folk Art Collection at Williamsburg, Virginia, Christmas, 1975. We would be remiss if we did not express our appreciation to the Antique Toy Collectors of America Club which, through its educational program, has reprinted a number of early toy manufacturers', jobbers', and distributors' catalogues. These materials have been an invaluable source of information.

Our thanks also to collector friends Harlan Anderson, Al Davidson, Dave Davidson, Lloyd Ralston, and Herbert Siegel, for sharing their knowledge, and to Howell Heaney of the Rare Book Department of the Free Library of Philadelphia.

To the President of Harry N. Abrams, Inc., Andrew Stewart, who first conceived the idea of this book; to Digby Diehl, who brought us together with Abrams; to Edith Pavese and Lory Frankel, our patient, understanding editors; and to Nai Chang, Abrams' Art Director, whose design talent was so important to this book, our grateful thanks.

B. M. B.

THE BARENHOLTZ COLLECTION

It all started in a somewhat unusual way: I needed a birthday present for my wife. After many years of selecting family gifts, like so many husbands and fathers I had run out of ideas. During a discussion with our children, I found out that on the way to the pediatrician's office with their mother some days before, they had seen some very attractive early American tin toys in an antique shop on Third Avenue in New York City. The suggestion was unusual, and yet, we *were* in the toy business and my wife did like antiques. We agreed on the blue tin milk wagon she had so admired. The birthday present was a great success!

There was no intent to collect at that time; the wagon was simply an attractive and decorative piece. We admired the workmanship; we speculated on the children who might have played with it, on other kinds of toys children of the nineteenth century had enjoyed, on the factories in which they had been made; but for the moment we were content simply to find a companion piece for the milk wagon. That was about twenty-three years ago: we were embarked on a twofold program—the active pursuit of our new hobby and research on the manufacturers and historical background of the toys we acquired.

Like most beginning collectors we had a great deal to learn. We bought inexpensive toys; some had a broken wheel, some were missing a driver or other part, on some the paint was worn; low cost was part of their attraction. We felt we would eventually find the missing part, and then we would find a skilled craftsman to make the necessary repairs. This never happened; some of the first toys we bought are in the collection today, the wheel still broken, the driver still missing, the repairs never made.

We were buying with little regard for type, material, or origin. Then a well-established collector advised us that we would do better to have fewer toys but to find "the best your money can buy. It is better to have one outstanding example for that twenty dollars than a group of inferior ones." That is still good advice.

Toys had been fairly easy to find in the 1950s. Our collection built up so quickly that we were not only running out of space but also out of money that could reasonably be spent on a hobby. Because we felt strongly that a collection was meant to be lived with,

13

not stored, we were faced with a decision: What direction should the collection take? What limits needed to be set?

We seemed to lean toward early American, partly due to our interest in folk art. Although the market abounded in beautiful foreign toys, we soon realized that American toys from the mid-1800s through the turn of the century, even those that imitated European design, were beautifully and soundly made in a wide variety of materials: tin, lead, britannia ware, cast iron, leather, rubber, wood, painted or lithographed. This was not really surprising since in America we have always produced a great variety of almost any manufactured product. Not only were the materials varied, but the toys were made in every category: bell toys, transportation toys, dolls, animals—from beetles in Noah's Arks to rocking horses—push and pull toys, balls, marbles, hoops, tops, squeak toys, musical toys, puzzles, games, mechanical and still banks, and all the others—about the same categories that continue to be produced today. The decision was difficult. Aside from an irresistible flight into robots, the collection is fairly representative of American toys, the majority having been produced between 1860 and 1900.

Why collect old toys? There are many different reasons and each collector has his own. Some enjoy collecting now because they had so few toys during their childhood; some still yearn for a particular toy once longed for in silence; some collect because they have a strong interest in the history and research involved. Some are compulsive accumulators; some have come to consider toys a good investment. I collect because of a long interest in the design and production of toys and a strong interest in history. Of course, the most important reason may not be intrinsic to the toys themselves, but to the wonderful people we have met all over the world, whose paths would probably never have crossed ours but for the sharing of this special interest in antique toys.

Today the beginning collector is eager to have guidelines to good collecting; the price of antique toys has skyrocketed, which makes trial and error a little more difficult and much more expensive. Over the years, I have formed a few basic guidelines that have been helpful to me. A great dealer, Frank Ball of Cambridge, Massachusetts, once impressed on me the importance of knowing with whom I was dealing; knowing your source is of the utmost importance. I think that next is to collect things that are available and reasonable; there *are* a few such toys left. Learn about toys; know that seeing and touching are active and important, a major way to learn about the age and condition of the toy. Train yourself to see form, shape, and texture. Expect to make some mistakes; consider them as part of your education as a collector. Again, buy the best quality toys available; one remarkable toy is more satisfying and worth more in the end than several ordinary ones. Lastly, always believe that there is a treasure over the next, or the next, hill.

The Barenholtz Collection has come a long way since the day I bought that birthday tin milk cart. In common with all collectors I have a list of some things I hope some day to find. In my search for these particular treasures, which I may or may never find, the collecting of toys is filled with excitement and rewards, often with great disappointment, but it is offset by the interesting people I meet along the way. Many of these people ask if the serious toy collector is any different from any other collector. I do not think so: theoretically it is only the objects collected that make a difference. Most collectors are dreamers, sometimes compulsive but incredibly patient and persistent in the pursuit of a desired object...and thereby hangs a tale.

Early to Rise...

A New York City store featuring antique toys advertised the sale of a well-known collection; none were to be sold before the announced opening time, 9:30 A.M.; no wheeling and dealing in advance. Because the sale was so widely publicized it was certain that collectors from all over the country would be there. I had seen the collection and remembered one particular toy—one of the treasures over the hill that I had always hoped to find. Abruptly our initiation period was over. We knew that toy collecting was not just a hobby; it was a hard-nosed business. I had no choice, if I wanted this particular toy, but to be among the first arrivals at the sale. This meant leaving Princeton, New Jersey, by 5:30 A.M. I arrived at 7. I was the first in line and spotted Santa in the window. By 9:30 the queue was about one hundred collectors long. When the door opened I avoided the rush as best I could and went directly to the shelf in the window where I had seen Santa in Sleigh with Goats.

As I examined it the details were not quite as I had remembered them and to myself I questioned the correctness of the toy. I was well aware of the rumors about this collection: the current owner had been known to repaint, to make repairs so skillfully as to be undetectable, even to own some toys that had been made of "married parts," the collectors' term for a toy made up of pieces that had not originally belonged together. So I deliberated: Where was a sleigh ever pulled by goats? Why not reindeer?

The closest examination I could make revealed that the goats fitted perfectly on the shaft. The soldering was old; it did not appear to have been touched. But crepe paper clothes for Santa? I knew of some European toys that had figures dressed in crepe paper. The more closely I examined it, the more European the Santa figure began to look. The sleigh was definitely American: the type of paint and the technique of soldering on the goats were similar to work on toys attributed to Althof, Bergmann, and since detachable figures are often missing or broken, it was possible that the Santa was not the original figure. Other collectors were eyeing the toy; a decision was imperative. It was such a rare toy, in such good condition, it would be worth having even if the Santa figure were a replacement. And so I made my purchase.

The next step was researching the Santa figure. Catalogues were checked, collectors queried, all to no avail. The seller was positive it was the correct figure; at least, he claimed, "That's what was there when I bought it." Four years later we heard of a duplicate. On comparing this with ours we found that they were indeed identical—goats, crepe paper clothing, and all. This is a treasured toy in the collection and, in retrospect, I feel much better about having gotten up at 5:30 to be the first in line at a toy sale.

...And Miles to Go...

Very early on I heard of a collector of mechanical banks in Pennsylvania. I had no real interest in banks at the time, but I did have an interest in meeting other collectors. I phoned and made an appointment—collectors seem to have an open door for each other and are generally interested in sharing experiences.

The people were charming and very knowledgeable about mechanical banks *and* toys. They collected the toys mostly for trading with toy collectors for mechanical banks. As is often the case, none of their toys were for sale, but they were interested in trading. Being relatively new collectors with no mechanical banks, this let us out. But there before our eyes, standing alone on a shelf, sat the largest and certainly the most beautifully made tin toy existent: the "Charles" Hose Reeler.

We admired and wanted the toy but it seemed quite unlikely that we could ever find a bank unusual enough to work out a trade. I asked what they knew about the background of the toy. The answer was that they had never considered it a toy; it was probably a salesman's sample and, as such, was the only piece in their collection that could be bought outright. It found a permanent home in our collection, but it was not quite at home, because we were always careful to point out to visitors that while it looked like a toy, it probably had been a salesman's sample.

A few years later the George Brown Sketchbook was added to our collection. This was the Connecticut tin manufacturer's sketching pad, the original drawings for the toys in his 1870 line. The most unusual aspect of the book was that the drawings were full-sized, the actual size of the toys. Among the sketches was—you guessed it—a Hose and Reel fire engine, the exact dimensions of Charles, with all the intricate details of design. It is now definitely established that Charles was produced as a toy, and I am still expecting that other great finds like Charles will turn up.

Some of Your Best Friends Won't Sell...

Often the piece you want most, even if it exists, cannot be bought from another collector, but if you have something to trade, it may well be negotiable.

For many years we had been looking for a Two-Seated Brake. Among the toys we most enjoyed at the time were cast-iron carriages, in any style, the two-seated brake being the most desirable in my opinion. I had seen only two, and those were in private collections, equally prized by their owners. About seven years ago I heard of one, bought at a Pennsylvania flea market, then traded to a mechanical bank collector. While he said he *liked* the brake, I sensed no great enthusiasm in his voice. It was not for sale, *but—* what duplicate did I have in my mechanical bank collection to trade? His collection was of long standing and quite complete; I had little hope of having anything on his want list. Still, I did have one very desirable and hard-to-find Roller Skating Bank which I had bought just for this purpose. Luck was with me; he did not own a Roller Skating Bank! We made the exchange, a peculiarly happy one for me.

The One You Came Home With...

In 1959 I attended a Maryland State Teachers' Convention, displaying educational materials for Creative Playthings, Inc. After driving all day and setting up the exhibit, I was ready for an early supper, some reading, and sleep. After supper I did read for a little while and then fell asleep, but it didn't last long. I tossed and turned until finally I gave up and turned on the light to read the local paper. I went through it in detail; I finished the book I had brought along. I still could not go back to sleep. I picked up the telephone directory and turned to the listing "Antiques" in the Yellow Pages. To my amazement there was a listing for "Antique Toys." I could hardly wait until nine in the morning when most shops open. My phone call was greeted with the recorded message, "The number you have reached is not a working number." I tried the alternate number. A woman answered and told me, "The shop has gone out of business and my husband has taken a job. He'll be home at six-thirty if you want to call then."

When I phoned, promptly at six-thirty, I had a warm, friendly response to my questions about his former shop and inventory. He was a collector, so many of the toys went back into his collection. He invited me to stop on my way home to see the toys he had. We spent a most enjoyable evening, with good collectors' talk, during which I described a tin fire-engine pumper I was anxious to find. He was not interested in tin toys, but he had seen just such a pumper at a dealer's shop a few weeks back. This sounded too good to be true. It was now 11:30 P.M. and he suggested calling the dealer. I was anxious to get the pumper, but it seemed late to impose on the dealer. I was assured that there would be no problem. He phoned, only to learn that the toy had been sold to another dealer whose name he gave me. In no way could I leave this hot trail, so I checked back into the motel for another restless night.

It now seems as if I must have been on that dealer's doorstep at sunrise. He finally arrived at 10:10. I introduced myself and said I had come to look at the tin fire engine he had. Fire engine? Oooh, yes! He *had* had one for a few days, a beauty too, but he had sold it the day before. As he described it I became more and more depressed because there was no doubt it was the one I had been searching for. Had it gone to another dealer? I asked hopefully, for then there might still be a chance for me to get it. No, it had gone to a collector in Philadelphia. That took care of the fire engine.

He invited me into the shop to see the toys he had. I was so disappointed I could not have cared less, but I went in. There were some Buddy L trucks, some dollhouses, some repainted cast-iron wagons, and some fire engines, none of which interested me at the time. I thanked him and asked that if any early tin of the quality of the fire engine ever turned up again to please let me know, to telephone collect. Agreed.

Just as I was leaving I noticed a door to the stock room slightly ajar and asked if he minded my taking a quick look. It was okay with him but he assured me there were no toys there. I walked in. What looked like the tip of a tin flag that might be on a toy was just visible, in a box of things under the wrapping counter. To my great delight I found that it *was* a flag, atop the Hull and Stafford semimechanical carrousel toy with soldiers and horses. I asked if it was for sale. Of course! He had forgotten he had it! My depression vanished; the chase had not been a disaster after all. Over the years I have seen only a few other toys similar to this, so when I think of how it was acquired, this Revolving Parade Pull Toy seems to assume a more important place in the collection.

It Pays to Be Friendly

Many years ago I had a call from a collector of electric trains. Did I have any? No, and I really didn't have any interest in them, but I did have some early tin clockwork trains and a few cast-iron ones. His only interest was in electric trains, but he asked to come by the next time he was in the Princeton area.

About three weeks later he was at a flea market nearby, phoned, and came over. We had a pleasant visit although our interests were quite different. He kept looking at one of the cast-iron trains and seemed intrigued even though it was not electric. As he was leaving he asked if I wanted to sell it. When I said no, he asked if I would have any interest in a tin boat he had just picked up at the flea market. Early tin boats were already hard to find; if it was of any interest perhaps we could work out a trade. What he brought in was the beautiful "Columbia" ferryboat. The cast-iron train immediately became available for a trade. I know of only three other ferryboats like this one.

Promise Me Roses But Bring Me Uncle Sam on a Tricycle

I believe the Uncle Sam on Velocipede to be one of the rarer clockwork toys made by Ives (Bridgeport, Connecticut). Aside from photographs in an early Ives catalogue, I had seen only one, in a collection in Paris. At that time I asked the usual collector's question—was it for sale? or trade? Inasmuch as it was so rare I received the expected answer, no, it was not.

About six years ago there was a toy swap meet held at a Pennsylvania motel. We were late in arriving, only to find that an Uncle Sam on Velocipede in very good condition had changed hands. The buyer had packed everything and was ready to leave so we could not even see it. Besides, while they had little interest in clockwork toys, both he and his wife had fallen in love with Uncle Sam. They were good friends and they assured us that while they had had many offers they had made no commitment and that if it were ever to be sold, we would be given first refusal.

Several years passed. Then he telephoned to say that he had a day off and would like to bring Uncle Sam over to Princeton for a visit. I too took the day off. As I saw Uncle Sam carried into my house, I knew I had to try to keep him there. My work was cut out for me. As we talked over lunch it came out that the owners had recently acquired another equally fascinating toy and were ready to relinquish Uncle Sam. He mentioned several cash offers he had had, one of which was astronomical. My heart fell.

I could see Uncle Sam pedaling back to Maryland because I was not prepared to meet that figure.

However, he had not accepted that offer because he preferred to trade it, if I were willing, for a cast-iron piece for his collection and a toy with a doll character that he could bring to his wife. My hopes brightened. We went into the gallery to see what would be interesting to them and still be a fair exchange. It took almost five hours of intensive negotiation but we finally arrived at a mutually agreeable exchange. The search for Uncle Sam certainly had carried us far and had had its ups and downs, but that's the way it sometimes is when a collector decides seriously that he wants a particular toy. The Maryland collector had gone a long way, but he had kept his promise to let me know when the toy became available. He left pleased with the addition to his and his wife's collections; Uncle Sam on Velocipede has a place of honor in my collection.

Law For Collectors: Leave No Stone Unturned

A Maryland antiques dealer friend has his business card imprinted with "One man's trash is another man's treasure." This is certainly true; some of the great toy finds were on their way to, or already in the city dump when they were discovered by a picker or collector. The history of the Lady in the Horse-drawn Sleigh is a good example. About ten years ago I heard about what sounded like a wonderful and varied collection that included some toys. The only tangible clue was the name of the small town in Pennsylvania where the unknown collector lived. That was all I had to go on. It was a long drive from Princeton but I started out to see what I could find. I inquired at the usual places—the local gas station, the post office, the town library—but no one had ever heard of anyone in town whose collection included toys. Even the antique dealers were nonplussed. One mentioned that the local garbage collector sometimes brought in things to sell, that he had on occasion found a toy, but so far as he knew, the man collected only the garbage.

It was frustrating to have come all this distance for nothing, but I had only myself to blame for setting out with so little information. I started home, stopping on the way for coffee and to reflect further on my stupidity; this time my pursuit of toys had been unreasonable. Then the collector in me got the upper hand and I decided that I really was not ready to give up. If the garbage collector brought toys to an antique dealer to sell, he must have some idea of their value. Perhaps *he* might know who had a toy collection, or might agree to call me if he ever again found a good antique toy. It was worth a try. I went back to the antique dealer, who gave me the name and address of the garbage collector. He also assured me that I was wasting my time, and I could see in his eye the pitying look reserved for the demented collector.

None daunted, I located the house. In response to my ring a man of about seventy-five years of age appeared, wearing then-old-fashioned gold-rimmed glasses and smoking a long cigar. I told him my story. He smiled pleasantly enough and said he hoped he could help. However, we did our talking on the front porch. He questioned me carefully,

19

asking who I was, where I had come from, why I had come to him, and how I had heard about this collector. I answered, patiently at first and then perhaps with waning interest: either he just liked to talk or he was pumping me to see if I could be of any value to him. At that point, he invited me into the house. The living and dining rooms showed no evidence of antiques or collections. We sat again and this time he asked me, "Do you know why I asked you all those questions?" and then proceeded to tell me that *he* was probably the collector I was looking for and that he preferred local people to be unaware of his interests. "I don't want to be bothered with people wanting to buy or sell." I had to smile and we had a good laugh about the whole affair.

He then said, "I will show you things that I have collected over many years with one stipulation: The first time you ask if anything is for sale, you leave." I assured him that I was happy to have found him and would like just to see his collection; that I enjoyed seeing things other people collected and often learned from just looking. Room after room was filled with every conceivable kind of collectible: watch fobs, political memorabilia, silver, pewter, and so many other things that I cannot remember, except for one room, filled to the brim with marvelous toys. There were steam toys, some tin toys, and a great many cast-iron toys. Even though nothing was for sale, it had turned out to be a wonderful day. The tracking down of an unknown collector, hearing how he built his collection from things that others had put out in their trash cans was an exciting and worthwhile experience.

About six months later I was in the area on business and phoned him. I had brought photographs of some of my collection which I thought he might like to see. He would; and why didn't I plan to come over that evening? This time I had a warm and cordial reception and I knew that I had a new collector friend. As the evening went on he said he had been thinking of selling a few things; he asked if I would be interested. Of course I would and I went home with several beautiful toys that had originally been destined for the town dump—including the Lady in the Horse-drawn Sleigh, made in Lancaster, Pennsylvania, in the latter part of the nineteenth century.

Research Brings Its Own Rewards

Serious toy collectors are usually interested in the history of the toy: where it came from, who made it, and so on. An interest in early American tin toys and a dearth of information about their history stimulated our research of the tin toy manufacturing industry in the United States, from about 1830 to 1890. Some information was available about several Philadelphia tin manufacturers, but not much was known about those in Connecticut. While researching George W. Brown and Company of Forestville, Connecticut—a producer of some of the nicest early tin toys—I came across the Merriam Manufacturing Company, in nearby Durham, a manufacturer of housewares and stationers' items with a seasonal line of toys as well. Since the Merriam Manufacturing Company was still in business in Durham it seemed both a logical and a simple matter to find out about the toys they manufactured.

Mrs. Barenholtz was doing most of the research so she went to Durham to talk to the owners. They had some background information and a few of the early molds and patterns but nothing else. The Durham Historical Society had a few toys on display. Its library had one early catalogue which it let us photograph as a working copy. We learned there of a man in town whose family had been part of the early company. He was very helpful and told what he knew about the history of the company as it had been repeated to him over the years. When asked if by chance he had any of the Merriam toys, without a word he went to a closet and produced a box with a jumble of toys. From them he carefully selected an enchanting Rabbit-in-Hoop. This was a first for us. We had never seen one; no collector we knew had ever made mention of such a toy. There were animals in hoops made by all the tin toy manufacturers, but to our knowledge never a rabbit. This was a rare find and of course brought the usual question, was it for sale?

No, it wasn't; all the toys in that box were kept for his grandchildren to play with when they came to visit. They loved the Rabbit-in-Hoop and enjoyed playing with it so it meant more to him than any of the others. It was a very friendly visit and we kept in touch: when the research was completed we sent him a copy of the book; for several years there was an exchange of Christmas greetings. The Christmas of 1973 a small package arrived in the mail. Attached on the outside was Mr. Newton's Christmas card. It read, "I have heard about your serious illness so I am sending your friend The Rabbit-in-Hoop to keep you company and make you feel much better." The rabbit fulfilled his mission and he remains a very important and cherished part of the Barenholtz Collection.

HISTORICAL BACKGROUND

Toys, and play to a lesser extent, have come a long way since the first little cave boy threw a stick at an animal in imitation of his father. Today toys and play are firmly established as integral parts of the emotional, mental, physical, and social development of the child. This is a recent development in the history of man.

The word "toys" as we use it today, meaning exclusively playthings for children, was not in common use until the nineteenth century. Up to this time and even into the early 1800s the word "toy" was used to describe anything from an adult bauble or gewgaw of little or no value, a trifle, to a costly miniature such as a piece of silver furniture made by the finest silversmith of the day.

The toys of today's children may be made of fantastically durable plastic or other synthetics but the shape and content have not changed very much over the years: toys still represent objects from the adult world to a great extent. Babies still get rattles, children still play with balls, dolls, hoops, stilts, tops—toys found in colonial America.

Babylonian, Egyptian, Greek, and Roman children all had balls, dolls, hoops, kites, marbles, stilts, and tops; some children had checkers and dominoes. New York's Metropolitan Museum of Art and other museums have in their collections toys from ancient Egypt, Greece, and Rome. Among them is an Egyptian rattle, estimated to be over two thousand years old. It is shaped like a cow, with small stones inside to provide the rattle. Were such rattles reserved for babies of the Pharaohs and the wealthy? How many Egyptian babies had one? No evidence remains to answer these queries. The museums also have examples of articulated toys from the same period: a baker, kneading his bread; a crocodile whose jaws open to snap up the unwary; a dog whose jaw moves up and down as if barking when its tail is raised or lowered. These are fairly sophisticated toys, made for amusement. It was a long time before such toys were again produced, even in Europe.

Centuries later, in 1658, one Jan Amos Komensky, better known by his Latin name, Comenius, had written *Orbis sensualium pictus*, said to be the first picture book intended for small children, translated the following year into English under the title *The Visible World*. Comenius, a Czech educator, advocated the use of concrete everyday objects—not toys—to help children learn from and within their environment.

From Comenius there is a direct line of educator/philosophers who concerned

Although unsigned, these paintings have been carefully researched and attributed to Joseph Whiting Stock. According to Stock's diary, the children are Mary and Francis Wilcox. A single, full-length portrait (48 x 40″) of the same two children, together with the bank and the doll, is in the collection of the National Gallery of Art in Washington, D.C. In that canvas, the children are holding each other's hands; the bank sits on the rug and the doll rests in a lovely red cradle.

Stock is believed to have painted the two separate three-quarter portraits, each 21 x 25″, from the single one about 1845. The girl wears a coral necklace. Besides making a pretty ornament, it was traditionally believed by the superstitious to ward off evil. The toys depicted and shown above each portrait were kept with the paintings. The china-head doll, of unknown manufacture, was made about 1845, and is 15½″ high. The pottery bank, made by Sheffield about the same time, is 5 x 6″.

The Cottage Bank, #84 in the George Brown catalogue, came with lock and key. Various tin toy manufacturers made cottage banks; this one is distinguished from the others by the gingerbread trim so widely used in Victorian architecture.

George W. Brown. 1880s. Tin, 5 x 6"

The carriages are counterparts of everyday carriages of the time—both are kinds of depot or delivery wagons.

Both toys: *Hull and Stafford. 1880s. Tin, length 9"*

themselves primarily with the human condition and the education of children. The teachings of Englishman Thomas Hobbes (1588–1679) dwelt on the theory that man was governable only because of his fear of death, which gave strong support to the Puritans' point of view. Then came John Locke (1632–1704). Despite being in disfavor with the government from time to time for his "radical views" he had an incalculable influence on the culture of his day, proclaiming that the child enters the world as a *tabula rasa*, not brutish or fearful but happy and reasonable, entitled to equal rights and the enjoyment of "life, health, liberty and possessions," so easily paraphrased in our Declaration of Independence by the words, "Life, Liberty, and the Pursuit of Happiness."

Jean Jacques Rousseau, with his emphasis on nature and environment, further promoted the idea of free development of human potential under self-imposed laws of reason. His principles are still influential in child psychology and education. Rousseau's *Emile* (1767) was probably read by some colonists, but before that, people had taken to Daniel Defoe's *Robinson Crusoe* (1719), in spite of its many long-winded passages of moralization. Before the end of the century these were deleted from children's editions. Paul Hazard, in his penetrating volume *Books, Children and Men* (1944), writes:

> Children like to destroy, we admit that; but they also like to build. Often, indeed, they destroy only to obtain material more to their taste. Building is one of their favorite games. They delight in building cardboard houses and wooden palaces, and nowadays automobiles, airplanes, and every kind of machine.... Good old Robinson Crusoe...shows them, each and every one, how they can build the world all over again to suit themselves.

It is interesting to note that in America, before the advent of the white man, Indian children had toys. Little girls had dolls. Some were made from cornhusks; some from a bit of wood—a torso with no legs—tapered on the end so that it could be held; some were faceless lest they steal the spirit of the child. In addition to small bows and arrows, Indian boys had leather balls stuffed with feathers that they tossed and caught and with which they played lacrosse and tetherball as it is played today. In 1585 the members of the Roanoke Expedition brought dolls in Elizabethan dress for the "natives" they expected to find. They also brought an artist, and in one of John White's sketches, made after the presentation of a doll, the little Indian recipient seems to know she has a toy.

In his diary of the crossing of the Atlantic in the *Arabella*, the Puritan John Winthrop wrote: "Games and horseplay with the seamen kept the young people's minds off their queasy stomachs." When the weather grew rougher, the captain "set our children and young men to some harmless exercises, which the seamen were very active in, and did our people much good, though they would sometimes play the wags with them." These entries indicate some play and freedom for the children of early settlers, however infrequent and if only from necessity, but play for the sake of amusement is nowhere mentioned.

Did some mother make room for a toy on board the *Mayflower* or the *Arabella*? Space was precious; much had been left behind; only the bare necessities went along. Was there room for a small toy? Was it hugged and taken to bed or would that have been sinful and depraved? Did it wear out? Was it ever copied according to the needlework ability of the mother or the skill of the father's carving? No evidence of anything so delightful has yet come to light.

One of the primary motives for the Puritans and Pilgrims to leave England was a strong desire to save their children from eternal damnation. This is borne out by the oft-quoted statement: "The Fountain of Learning and Religion were soe corrupted, in addition to the unbearable fees, most children even with the best witts and fairest hopes were perverted and corrupted by the multitude of evil examples and the licentious government of the schools they attended" (John Winthrop in *Reasons to Be Considered and Objections with Answers for Justifying the Undertakeres of the Intended Plantation in New England*, 1632).

Probably the main reason that the government of England finally allowed the Puritans and Pilgrims to leave was economic: they would not only colonize the new world but also help to meet England's expanding need for raw materials. However, the harsh climate, the total unpreparedness of the newcomers, the high death rate, and the hardships of their first years here deferred the purposes of both government and immigrants. There was little time for thought of economics, education, or play. The days were devoted to work and religion; survival was the goal, survival of body and soul.

Puritans believed their babies were born not merely ignorant, but, having inherited Adam's original sin, inescapably evil as well. It was important that their wills, particularly if strong or obdurate, be dutifully broken. Hence, Puritans constantly reminded their children of their innate iniquity and depravity. Jonathan Edwards, in a special children's sermon, preached, "Tis not likely you will all live to grow up. . . . God is very angry with you. How dreadful it will be to be in Hell among the devils and know that you must be there to all eternity." Cotton Mather recognized his children's birthdays but the only celebration recounted in his diary tells us: "I would make it an opportunity when the birthdayes of my several children arrive to discourse very proper and pungent things unto them, relating to their eternal interests. . . ." And while he may not have been "fond of proposing Play to them," obviously the idea *did* occur to him. In their *A Book of Americans* (1933), Rosemary and Stephen Vincent Benét characterized the Puritans:

> They didn't care for Quakers but
> They loathed gay cavaliers
> And what they thought of clowns and plays
> Would simply burn your ears
> While merry tunes and Christmas revels
> They deemed contraptions of the Devil's.

In the 1650s, when life in the colonies was still very difficult, John Cotton, the minister, admitted that little children "spend much time in pastime and play, for their

The daguerreotype process was invented in France by Louis Daguerre in 1839. It was introduced into the United States by Samuel F. B. Morse of telegraph fame and his coworker John Draper.

The two children took this portrait-sitting very seriously. The younger child is holding some kind of rattle. The older one holds a water trow, made by George Brown and by Stevens and Brown in the early 1870s. The daguerreotype and the toy were kept together—by someone who either saved everything or had a canny sixth sense about the future of tin toys.

25

This young boy appears to be dressed in a homemade suit; his high button shoes suggest the 1870s or 1880s. He holds a tin hose reel carriage, probably made by Hull and Stafford.

bodies are too weak to labour, and their minds to study are too shallow...even the first seven years are spent in pastime, and God looks not much at it" (*Practical Commentary or An Exposition...upon the First Epistle of John*, 1656). And Benjamin Wadsworth in his *Well-Ordered Family* (1712) wrote, "Time for lawful Recreation now and then is not altogether to be denied them....Yet for such to do little or nothing else but play in the streets, especially when almost able to earn their living is a great sin and shame." The phrase "almost able to earn their living" referred to seven- or eight-year-olds.

For all their religious fervor, Puritan parents, surely fearful themselves seeing only four out of ten children reach their teens, were not physically cruel to their children. Cotton Mather instructed tutors to "Be Strict, But yet Gentle too....The Lads with Honour first, and Reason Rule;/Blowes are but for the Refractory Fool." As for his own children, his diary reveals "The First Chastisement, which I inflict for an ordinary Fault, is, to let the Child see and hear me in Astonishment, and hardly able to believe that the Child could do so base a Thing, but beleeving that they will never do it again. I would never come to give a child a Blow; except in the Case of Obstinacy; or some gross Enormity."

Living in the new England was a far cry from the small settled towns of the midlands from which the Puritans and the Pilgrims had come. In spite of the God-fearing rigidity of the parents, the children perforce learned "from and within their environment." Occasionally the men went sailing; sometimes a boy must have been allowed to go along. They went hunting and fishing as an almost daily part of their food procurement routine, and boys of ten to twelve years *did* go along. These activities provided some respite from toil and prayer. Some of the men played bowls on the village green; surely the children must sometimes have watched—or even played! There were occasional bow-and-arrow shooting matches. In the main, happiness was to be found in family gatherings. Life was not all tears, prayers, and work, but if there were any toys there are none of record.

The severity of the Puritans' life was reflected in their clothing. Puritan clothes were simple, layered against the cold. Women's and children's clothes were stiffened to support the back through long hours of heavy work and to maintain straight posture. Infants of both sexes were dressed in swaddling clothes, synonymous with no opportunity for movement. When freed of this impediment, both boys and girls wore ankle-length dresses. They all wore a "Gertrude," a coarse smock, linen in warm weather, wool in winter; they often wore a coif indoors. All these clothes were somewhat restricting. Perhaps the clothing made it easier for infants to bear their need to be silent and obedient; customs and costumes often fit the times. At six or seven boys were "breeched" and some children actually had scarlet ribbons, even though rich dress was forbidden by law, except for the wealthy, for dress was a sign of class.

Once survival was assured, the settlers had time to think of educating their children. Many learned to read at home, taught by parents and siblings; others learned by doing during the daily responsive religious family readings. One of the first schools, with one room and one master, was established in Boston in 1635 "for the teaching and nurturing of children with us." By 1700 most towns had set up schools, from a dame's group for little ones to public schools. There were also church schools and tutors, both of which were private. There are records showing that children were not admitted to the Boston public schools until they were seven, but then "the children of every class of citizens" associated freely. In some schools, girls remained for five years and boys for seven; in others, both remained until they were fourteen. School was serious business; there were no such things as educational toys.

While most of the colonists in New England were of homogeneous Anglo-Saxon stock, the settlers to the south, in New York, New Jersey, Delaware, and especially Pennsylvania, had widely varied origins, customs, and religions. They included Dutch, Finns, French, Germans, Moravians, Quakers, and more, almost all without any attachment to England or Puritanism. Children lived in a warmer climate, both physically and socially. Still further south, particularly among the affluent, children's lives were even easier. Parents who could afford a nurse or a slave to take care of the children surely found it far easier to enjoy them. According to New Englanders and foreigners who traveled through the South, the children were "spoiled" and "indulged." Literature on child rearing was appearing wherever books were sold. Children were being looked at in a new light. The winds of change had started to blow; there was no possibility of reversing them.

From about 1725 on, playthings could be found throughout the colonies: not novelties, but toys that reflected the child's environment, toys to play with, to use, and to enjoy. Some colonial babies, like their cousins in England, had rattles. Some were made of wood, whittled at home or carved by a local artisan; some were made of silver with bells or a whistle, imported from England. These were usually attached to a stick of coral, good "to ease the pain of teething." Those of silver were expensive treasures; a bill in existence shows that Martha Washington bought a silver rattle for a grandchild at a cost of twenty-five dollars. From an earlier date (1759) there is a copy of George Washington's Christmas list of presents for his stepchildren, five-year-old John and three-year-old Patsy:

A bird on Bellows	A Tunbridge Tea Sett
A Cuckoo	3 Neat Tunbridge Toys
A turnabout Parrot	A Neat Book fash Tea Chest
A Grocers Shop	A box best Household Stuff
An Aviary	A straw Patch box w. a Glass
A Prussian Dragoon	A neat dress'd Wax Baby
A Man Smoakg	

A "bird on Bellows" was a squeak toy available here; the "Tea Sett," "3 Neat Toys," and the "neat dress'd Wax Baby" would have had to be imported, possibly from the Royal Tunbridge Fair. "Man Smoakg (Smoking)" was a mechanical toy, either French or English. The "Grocers Shop" might have been made here but was probably imported

27

Someone brought these three lovely children to be preserved for posterity by the new daguerreotype process. The girl is holding a doll of the day; the infant is holding Mama's sewing case or some such object to keep her attention, and the boy is holding a Hull and Stafford tin Man on Horse in Hoop.

from Germany. Such a list would have represented a small fortune for the ordinary citizen and could have been assembled only by the head of a wealthy family.

Aside from dolls and balls, colonial children had other toys, such as bull-roarers. The first ones were made from wood, bone, or ivory. Fastened at one end or suspended by a leather thong from the hole in the middle, they were whirled or pulled rhythmically until they produced a whirring sound that was quite noisy and satisfying. One such toy, made from a William III coin, was found in the camp occupied by the British during the Revolutionary War, in what is now Fort Tryon Park in Upper Manhattan.

Colonial children also had a cup-and-ball toy, popular for centuries. (See Brueghel's painting *Children's Games;* it is fascinating and gives an excellent overview of toys and games of his day.) These were usually made of wood or ivory, and were plain, decorated, or carved. To toss the ball and get it back into the cup required considerable manual dexterity and was a favorite pastime. It is still available, often sold as a souvenir in American restoration villages so popular with tourists. Children also had battledore and shuttlecock, available today as badminton. They played with balls, dolls, hoops, kites, marbles, stilts, and tops. Some had checkers and some had dominoes. The hoops were made of metal or wood, to be rolled by hand or speeded up with a stick in the manner of children of ancient Greece and Rome. As today's child puts a card between the spokes of his bicycle to simulate the sound of an engine, so the boy from the Golden Age of Greece strung bells across the diameter of his hoop to jingle as he ran. Later the same hoops were made of the lightest wood, covered in velvet and bedecked with ribbons for girls and young ladies to play "Graces," each of the players tossing her hoop to the other simultaneously and trying to snare the opposing hoop on her small sticks. This game was still doing well in 1900 when it was issued by Parker Brothers under the name of Diavolo, "newly imported from Europe."

The colonists won the Revolutionary War but it was really not until after the War of 1812, with the Treaty of Ghent in 1815, that the gains won thirty years earlier were solidified and that internal dissension and European interference with American trade were resolved. Time had healed most of the wounds caused by division of loyalties and separation of families and friends during the Revolutionary War; universal suffrage—for men only—was spreading; the concepts of political and personal freedom and social equality were slowly becoming realities. Children too began to enjoy a measure of the new-found freedom.

The Revolutionary leaders, Washington, Jefferson, and the Adamses, had urged the development of an informed electorate. At least partial fulfillment was on the horizon: public schools by the thousands were being established throughout the populated parts of the country, supported by taxes as opposed to church schools supported mainly by tuition and the free services of teachers. Large numbers of children were in attendance. The resulting crops of readers encouraged not only the founding of newspapers but the writing of books for children. These were still moralistic but there was some variety in the stories and there was a choice of titles. Printed board games and playing cards became acceptable family diversions; eventually they too were designed for children and advertised in the weekly papers (there were few dailies) along with an increasing number of items made specifically for children, including some toys.

The Victorian Age was an age of mottoes, of the Golden Rule, but also of "Do as I say, not as I do." It was an age in which many people of the poor, lower classes molded their child-rearing behavior on the patterns of the middle class, pursued middle-class ethics, and tried to live middle-class lives without middle-class incomes, a continual "trying to keep up with the Joneses" kind of life. "Children should be seen and not heard" was another maxim of the era. Rules of conduct were still closely drawn and children simply measured up. Most attended Sunday School, said their prayers at night before going to bed, and did what they were told, when they were told, without question.

In spite of increased leisure and freedom each member of the family retained a designated role, a share of responsibility; children too had their responsibilities and were expected to meet them. In addition, everyone in the community knew everyone else; neighbors were often like members of an extended family; standards of behavior were clearly defined and generally accepted by all. It made bringing up children much easier.

While social changes were slow in coming, economic changes came at an incredible pace. It was an age of extremely rapid growth and expansion; an age of prosperity, freedom, and security; an age of great adventure (the Gold Rush) and small wars (with Mexico and Spain) which the young country won. There was a tremendous influx of immigrants, at first from the northern European countries, among them people whose trade was already that of toy maker, and who in all probability made the same types of toys on arrival here that they had been making before they left Europe.

First- and second-generation Americans were running small tin and wood turning shops and finding the manufacture of toys a profitable sideline. The tin makers were chiefly in Connecticut and Pennsylvania, the woodturners in Pennsylvania, Rhode Island, and New York, where Jesse Crandall was dubbed "The Child's Benefactor" because he designed and manufactured toys that engaged the child's interest and spirit of play. People were beginning to go to the shore, and Crandall's small sand molds became the rage. Children were no longer forced to learn the alphabet by rote to the accompaniment of punishment for errors; letters could be molded at the beach or in sand sold for use in the home! Simple blocks were being mass-produced, blocks with which children could build while they absorbed the names of the animals and letters pictured on the sides.

In the 1830s, farming was the chief occupation in the United States, with almost every farmer owning his own land and making his living from it. At the time that many of the toys in this collection were manufactured, the South—approximately one-half the country—was raising only cotton or tobacco, mostly on plantations with slave labor, some of which were extensive and owned by very wealthy families. There were no farms of comparable size in the North, where few farmers were rich. In fact, Marshall Davidson, in vol. 1 of *Life in America*, characterizes the small-scale New England farmer as self-sufficient but "quite likely an illiterate and ill-nourished member of society."

Did the poor child on the right come to be photographed in these clothes or did the photographer provide the flowing tie and artist's smock two sizes too big for him? Did he bring his favorite tin toy—White Horse Gig—or was this one of the photographer's props? There are no answers to these questions. The patterned tablecloth and chair *do* look like studio fixtures.

The toy (pictured on page 125) was made by Stevens and Brown about 1870.

29

Just as the lives of laborers, toy makers, and blue- and white-collar workers were revolutionized by technical advancements, the exploding population, and westward expansion—all creating new markets and new jobs—so the farmers' lives were undergoing rapid and earthshaking changes.

New, efficient laborsaving machines (the cotton gin, the reaper, and a host of others) made it possible for farmers to expand their holdings, even with fewer workers, so that many farms were raised from subsistence level to one comparable with business. Uncle Sam was interested in his farmers, an interest expressed in cartoons like "The World Is My Market." The Uncle Sam Mechanical Bank must have promoted thrift among farm as well as city children.

Dickens has written copiously on the children of the Victorian Era, American as well as English (he visited and traveled here in 1842 and again twenty-five years later). He portrayed the children as pathetic, left to their own devices, with the odds for survival strongly against them. In his fiction he crusaded against neglect and cruelty to children. He focused on the fears of childhood—fear of the dark; fear of being whipped, punished, sent to bed without supper; of being shut up in closet or cellar; fear that parental love would be taken away.

The mortality rate was still high among children; the use of vaccines was rare, doctors were scarce, and pediatricians scarcely heard of. Deathbed scenes were dramatic and funerals melodramatic. Many young boys and girls were working long hours, in textile mills, in coal and tin mines, in city sweatshops, and on farms; many, boys in particular, went to school only when their labor was not required at home. There was a great deal of poverty. In *Progress and Poverty* (1880), Henry George wrote that trying to meet the rent in poor families "takes little children from play and from school and compels them to work before their bones are hard or their muscles firm." In his role as social worker trying to effect change in the mean, drab lives of poor city children, Jacob Riis photographed his famous "street arabs" of the New York City slums in the 1880s and '90s. There are no toys in the pictures, not even broken ones taken from trash heaps.

Today we are well into the second generation of children for whom the Laura Ingalls Wilder books have been a much-read chronicle of pioneer childhood in America, a period that nearly parallels the dates of these toys. The Wilders had four daughters, each of whom had a homemade doll, of wood or corncob. Laura herself remembered having some pangs of envy over a playmate's china-head doll. One particularly entertaining toy was a kind of battledore made of a pig's bladder, dried and attached to a stick to be batted about; a chicken foot with the tendons left in made an ingenious mechanism that opened and closed as the tendons were pulled; and there is a glowing account of one miraculous birthday when Pa whittled a jumping jack for Laura. No "boughten" toys at all.

The world of literature opened up for the children of the Victorian Era, literature written especially for them, including periodicals; *Chatterbox, St. Nicholas,* and *Youth's Companion* were among the most widely circulated. Many stories focused on heroic deeds, on the choice between right and wrong, both of which were very clearly defined. Evil suffered prompt and just punishment, while good, praised and sometimes rewarded, was more or less a matter of noblesse oblige.

By mid-century the diversity in religions was weakening the moralist hold of the Calvinists and the Puritans over children. Among adults, small intellectual groups like the Brook Farm movement, transcendentalists who did not see God as a remote, punitive figure but as existing in and through man and nature, had a strong influence on adult literature and thought. How far it affected the lives of most of the children is a moot point.

Children's clothing had been simplified from copies of adult court dress, but the Victorians went back to buckram stiffening, redingotes, panniered skirts, and layers of starched petticoats. Women wore buns or rats to thicken the hair and whalebones to thin the waist. Toward the end of the era skirts for girls were shortened, but often as not pantalets with embroidered ruffles covered the limb to the ankle, or the skirt met the top of the boot. Pioneer and country children were less formally dressed except for church-going and important celebrations. *Godey's Lady's Book* and *Harper's Bazar* illustrated the fashions of the day.

One of the last fashion flings of the era was the Little Lord Fauntleroy velvet suit with lace collar, not so restricting from the viewpoint of physical comfort, but very restricting when one had to remember to keep clean and not tear one's suit. Far more comfortable and wearable were the copies of regulation sailor suits which many boys enjoyed wearing; the style remained popular until World War I. By 1900, ready-made clothes for adults, children, and dolls had taken the fancy of the American public.

Most handmade goods—home industries—were being displaced. As life grew easier, producing to meet people's needs became specialized. Craftsmen were becoming skilled mechanics, some of whom applied their aptitude for invention to toys. As the country prospered, leisure time increased; craftsmen were free to make occasional toys to amuse their children, then the neighbors' children, then to trade or sell. As water power shifted to steam, factories sprang up wherever power was available. Household goods, farm equipment, and such were being made by machines; they were also less durable. The artisan who had made the whole tin toy by himself, the stenciling done perhaps by wife or daughter, had all but vanished from the business scene; the jack-of-all-trades who had cushioned many discomforts and minor domestic crises (by mending pots and pans, for example) was also on his way out of the economic picture. There was less mending and more replacement. The first steps toward built-in obsolescence had been taken in an effort to keep the new mass production going all year long.

Small businesses began to boom; toy shops grew into small toy manufactories, particularly in the Northeast. The introduction of interchangeable parts led to the rapid development of one Connecticut factory that produced as many as half a ton of cast-iron toy wheels in one day. The availability of precision wheels of varied design and sizes enabled small shops to turn out handmade tin toys with a mass-produced-looking finish. Toys went quickly into motion: they were pushed and pulled; they bobbed up and down; they rolled. They began to have sound effects—at first rather gentle in the form of small bells but soon louder and noisier with gong bells and Centennial Freedom

The Whistler Locomotive is shown in front of the Ives factory in Bridgeport, Connecticut, where it was made.

31

Ringers and Liberty Bells. These action toys were replicas of the moving vehicles children saw in the world about them: pleasure wagons, traps, coaches, and buggies; service carts of all kinds such as peddlers' wagons, ice, coal, and grocers' wagons or drays, all drawn by horses. And, as fire companies were established, the several pieces of equipment used by the fire department were reproduced, no longer pulled by volunteers but by swift-running horses. The new cast-iron stoves, sad irons, and other housekeeping equipment were reproduced for girls. By mid-century the world of toys had joined the world of business.

This did not mean that toys were available everywhere to all children. Two knowledgeable and highly reputable observers of the day give these contrasting pictures of children and toys. William McGuffey, educator from Ohio, printed in his *Third Eclectic Reader* (1837) a conversation between a boy who stopped a runaway horse and its owner who wanted to give him a reward.

> *Mr. Lenox.* Thank you, my good boy, you have caught my horse very nicely....
>   If you had a dime now, what would you do with it?
> *Boy.* I don't know sir. I never had so much.
> *Mr. L.* Have you no playthings?
> *Boy.* Playthings? What are they?
> *Mr. L.* Such things as nine-pins, marbles, tops, and wooden horses.
> *Boy.* No sir. Tom and I play at football in the winter, and I have a jumping
>   rope. I had a hoop, but it is broken.
> *Mr. L.* Do you want nothing else?
> *Boy.* I have hardly time to play with what I have. I have to drive the cows, and
>   run of errands, and to ride the horses to the fields, and that is as good as play.

Whether the boy ever got a reward I do not know, but playing with toys as children do today was not part of his world.

The other side of the coin is detailed in an account of Henry Thoreau in *The Maine Woods* (1864). On August 31, 1846, Thoreau left Concord, Massachusetts, "for Bangor and the backwoods of Maine." Sixty-three miles north of Bangor he came upon a small store near the inn in which he had spent the night.

> Here was a little of everything in a small compass to satisfy the wants and the ambition of the woods—a stock selected with what pains and care, and brought home in a wagon box, or a corner of the Houlton team; but there seemed to me, as usual, a preponderance of children's toys—dogs to bark and cats to mew, and trumpets to blow, where natives there hardly are yet. As if a child, born into the Maine woods, among the pine cones and cedar berries, could not do without such a sugar-man, or skipping-jack, as the young Rothschild has.

At the beginning of the era many families had never set foot outside the villages in which they lived, but as turnpikes and toll roads were built, relay stops were being built at intervals along the way—stables where fresh horses could be hitched up while the traveler stretched and had some refreshment; one could take longer journeys without the expense and delay of stopping for the night. Slow and hard as it may seem to us, travel was becoming faster and more comfortable, and available to more people. The carriages and coaches that traveled the roads were reproduced by toy makers in tin and cast iron. Boats plied the rivers, goods were transported quickly and cheaply by water. One Connecticut toy factory, still in business a hundred years later, told how toys were hauled from the factory to the river dock by oxteams; the toys were loaded on the night boat and were in New York City in the morning, picked up or delivered to the store the same day. The toy oxteams and the boats, the delivery carts and the horses were made by that same factory and others nearby, and were among the toys that went down the Connecticut overnight.

Within only a few years, as business expanded, the wood- and tin-makers diversified their wares: the sled manufacturer working in wood made clothespins, sap buckets, backs for brushes—all calculated to keep the factories going on a year-round basis. The shop that made metal penny toys, tin or iron toys turned to making hardware, and vice versa; clock manufacturers made the mechanisms for mechanical toys. Money was available; business was good. Ocean-crossing time had been cut in half. (Although the first steamship crossing was made in twenty-nine and a half days from Savannah to Liverpool, this was still far outstripped by the beautifully rigged clippers which crossed in fifteen days by 1838.) By mid-century the screw propeller had been developed, replacing paddlewheels, making trade of goods and ideas with Europe easier. The new ships were reproduced as toys named after current heroes and sailed in park ponds in cities and on lakes and along rivers in the country—or in the new bathtubs at home.

There was now plenty of shipping room for imported luxuries; as is the case today, what had been considered a luxury at the turn of the century had become a necessity for succeeding generations. There was room for children's toys, so much room that early on Congress passed a protective tariff for the American toy industry—15 percent if the toys were transported in American ships and 16.5 percent if the vessels were foreign.

Very elaborate individual mechanical toys had been especially commissioned in Europe, particularly in France for the young princes of the royal family. News of these toys eventually reached the artisans. The Industrial Revolution enabled inventive minds to use new principles of engineering and facilitated the use of mechanical improvements in the making of toys.

In 1861, Milton Bradley, the Springfield, Massachusetts, toy maker, introduced child-oriented toys for kindergartens, aimed at teaching the child through play "the child's equivalent of the adult job." Kindergarten was the concept of Friedrich Froebel (1782–1852), who opened the first one in Germany in 1837. Froebel was also one of the first to offer educational toys especially made for children. He designed seven "gifts" which were not toys in our context at all. They were tools of learning, geometric shapes purposely designed to be used at specific stages in the child's development, intended to

George W. Brown made the side-wheeler "New York." It was photographed beside the Connecticut River in Forestville, where the toy company was located.

33

be entertaining in the sense of engrossing, but not strictly for pleasure. Bradley expanded Froebel's "gifts" from seven to twenty and sold the simply designed toys in his retail store in Springfield as well as through the Bradley catalogue.

Simple form and lack of detail have never hindered the very young child's fun or inhibited his creative expression; quite the contrary, they have stimulated and fostered his imagination. It is only as children get older that they enjoy the richness of detail, accurate scale, and realistic reproduction of the object manufactured as a toy. This is an important factor in the model field, where one company was enjoined by the United States government from producing certain battleships and submarines during World War II because the design and detail were too accurate. It is interesting to remember that in 1892 Milton Bradley was also restrained by the United States Government from making toy money, in particular, pennies that were too realistic.

Throughout the nineteenth century, the most important possession of a family was a horse: a horse to haul the wood to build the house; a horse to work the farm; horses to haul all the new wagons: trolleys, fire engines, coal, ice, and water wagons, U.S. mail carts and every sort of delivery cart, including peddlers' wagons with tinware and tin toys from Connecticut—each and every one drawn by a horse or two. In the case of an elegant family landau or a tallyho there were two or four beautifully matched horses; in addition there were sleek trotters and racehorses. In Victorian novels the status symbol of the dashing hero was an elegant equipage, a fast single pacer or trotter, a horse and carriage, or a "spanking pair of bays"; his counterpart from the farm sometimes could go courting in the farm buggy. All these pleasure vehicles, delivery carts, and horses were reproduced in the toy world, and the toy reproductions of the status symbols were as expensive by comparison as the real ones.

The beautiful four-dollar Carpenter Tally-ho, the Ives Mechanical Automatons at three dollars, the Freedom Bell Ringer at the same price, these and similarly priced toys were not for poor children, indeed not for the average child either. It is difficult to translate money value from one age to another, but in the 1870s, three to four dollars was a good weekly salary for many workers, decidedly on the high side for some. In 1889 a Francis W. Carpenter Company toy maker earned $8.50 for a 60-hour week. By assembling anywhere from twelve to thirty-six *dozen* toys a week, in his spare time, at five cents the dozen, his largest earnings totaled $10.30 for *one* week, according to a time sheet for that year. Whatever the value of the dollar, what family at any time can, should, would, does spend a week's or half a week's pay on a toy for a child? If it does happen—today, for a ten-speed bicycle in lieu of the Irish Mail of the 1880s, or for one's own television set instead of a family Zoetrope in the 1870s—how often does it happen? The Carpenter Tally-ho was for the child whose parents had a tallyho of their own in the carriage shed—not very many in the whole United States.

From this one can assume that at least some toys shown here have been preserved because of their original cost; bought for children who had many toys so that they suffered less wear and tear than if there had been only one or two toys. Then, too, there were the "downstairs" people and a nana or upstairs maid to keep the toys in order if the children did not. Andrew Carnegie chastised the newly rich families for "display and extravagance in home, table or equipage," and "for enormous sums ostentatiously spent," which extended to toys for their children. However limited the sale, there was a market for these expensive toys. Children in families of average means were likely to have had penny toys and ten- or twenty-five cent toys, in wood, tin, or cast iron.

The time span of these toys had seen great changes. In 1830 the United States was a fledgling among nations; in 1900 it was a world power. In 1830, had it occurred to anyone to cross the continent, he would have required great courage and stamina, a Conestoga wagon, and a near–Jules Verne mentality. By 1900 one could sleep one's nights away while crossing the country in a Pullman car and view the scenery from a vestibule car by day. These trains were translated into toy trains of wood, tin, and cast iron, push and pull, windup, and friction; then came tracks and steam; and by 1900 toy trains, like their mass transportation counterparts, were on the verge of electrification. There were travel books, map puzzles, travel games, and globes; Americans traveled all over the world and all of it was reproduced for their children.

Many people felt that they were working toward, and had some chance of achieving, better lives, better working conditions, if not exactly Utopia. They expected life to improve in the next generation, and material progress was made. Better still, the next generation was getting taller and healthier, having more schooling, more opportunities for advancement—and living longer.

Whereas the Census Bureau for 1850 had listed 47 toy makers, by 1880 it listed 173 toy and game manufacturers, not including carriage and sled makers. The volume of the toy business equaled that of the manufacture of telephone and telegraph apparatus; of paper collars and cuffs, sporting goods, brassware, and cleaning and dyeing. Unquestionably, by the turn of the century the United States was a first-class world power, trading freely all over the world, designing, manufacturing, importing, and exporting...children's toys.

TOYS TO GROW ON

Teething rings and rattles first—rattles for the infant to grasp, with which to make an exciting noise, causing the baby to wave its arms, thereby making more exciting noise. Then a soft object, to clutch and to feel, to drop and pick up, to drop and have someone else pick up—the early beginnings of playing "catch."

As soon as the infant gets on his or her feet, still not quite erect but tending to tilt forward and needing a goal of loving arms or some support, able to take only a few steps, a push toy is often enough to steady the new walker. When the push toy is a hoop with jingling bells it surely must encourage the child to take a few more steps. When it was a horse with a bell ringing, it must have been a joyful impetus, and must have made a joyous sound, the bells mingling with the delighted laughter of the child.

Then pull toys for the child who is erect and walking. What fun to make the bell pull toys go faster, or go in a circle, and, when tired, to be able to drop down on the floor and play with them. And, finally, blocks—blocks to stack one, two, and three high—and then the fantastic discovery that they can be knocked down, safely replaced, and knocked down again, supplying the endless repetition that leads to mastery. These are toys to grow on.

Alphabet Man

Although the Alphabet Man is a manufactured toy, it has the shape, proportion, and scale of a piece of folk art. The letters of the alphabet, in order, are located in the man's collar. As the child pressed the lever, the man's left hand pointed to an uppercase letter. Each time the lever was pressed, the next letter of the alphabet came into view. Obviously an educational toy, it is a great example of toys made for fun as well as for learning.

Maker unknown. 1880s. Cast iron, height 10"

Left: **Child with Teething Ring**

Joseph Whiting Stock. c. 1845. Oil on canvas, 30 x 25"

Left below: **Infant's Teething Ring**

The rhyme "Mary had a little lamb" is illustrated on the bell. Such teething rings were usually fastened to the carriage or bassinet with a blue or pink ribbon.

Maker unknown. Mid-1800s. Sterling silver (bell) and mother-of-pearl (ring), length 3"; ring: diameter 1"

Below: **Rattles**

Counterclockwise from bottom, left:

Small pebbles in the tin top cause the rattling. Air blown into the holes makes a high but pleasing sound; teeth marks around the holes indicate signs of use and excitement at a whistling sound which must have been quite difficult for a baby to produce at will.

Maker unknown. c. 1870. Bone and tin, length 5"

Although made from one block of maple, this rattle has five rings that slide freely up and down the spindle, creating a pleasant sound.

Maker unknown. Mid-1800s. Wood, length 6½"

The George Brown Sketchbook shows this rattle (#100) at $3 per gross (wholesale), as does the Stevens and Brown catalogue of 1872.

George W. Brown. 1870. Tin, length 5¼"

This rattle has a shallower drum for the noise box. It was manufactured in several different sizes, all with the patriotic eagle motif and "For a good child" on the reverse side; the alphabet is raised on the rim. The workmanship and material suggest that this too is a Brown product.

George W. Brown(?). 1870. Tin, length 5½"

The wooden, homemade rattle was a popular pattern and a challenge to the carver. It is sometimes found in puzzle form, without glue, interlocking tightly.

Folk art. Maker unknown. c. 1860. Wood, length 7"

Child with Rattle

This painting was done in Marblehead, Massachusetts. The initials "W. D." are on the painting. In the lower right corner is written, "Taken when 7 months old." Below is the date. The child is tied to the chair with her sash to keep her from falling.

Attributed to William Thompson Bartoll. 1838. Oil on canvas, with wood frame: 18 x 18"; unframed: 16 x 16"

Hoops

The push toy has been an important toy for many centuries. The push hoop is one of the favorites of infants beginning to walk. This toy was manufactured in several different versions, most making some kind of sound as they were rolled. Some were made with bells, others with spool-like pieces of wood and pieces of metal loosely fitted to the spokes so that the hoop would jingle as it was pushed or pulled.

Albert Hill of New Haven, Connecticut, was granted the patent *(left)* for a Rolling Hoop in 1871. The manufacturers of these hoops, all made in the 1870s, are unknown. The hoop on the left is 15½" in diameter with a 24"-long handle. There are traces on the spools of red paint with green striping. The wheel and handle are a natural finish. The center hoop is 20" in diameter with a 27" handle. The hoop on the left is 12" in diameter with a 20" handle.

40

Opposite: **Horse Pull Toy**

The workmanship of this toy and the metal hexagonal sign, a hand-cut six-pointed star, unquestionably point to a product of Pennsylvania, where the toy was found. The colors are typical of those on so many pieces of Pennsylvania Dutch folk art—fractur painting, tinware, and such—brown, green, and orange. The design is simple: a wire mechanism on a roller axle moves the platform up and down as the toy is pulled, creating the illusion of a galloping horse. This horse still has its tail, made of hemp.

Folk art. Maker unknown. c. 1880. Wood, 11 x 9½"

Infant's Ball

Is there anything really new under the sun? Present-day clutch balls, a first infant toy, are produced by several toy companies, usually made of polyurethane instead of this smooth velvet. If the two were placed side by side, were it not for the difference in texture one would be hard put to differentiate them by the shape.

The colors are now faded, but appear originally to have been bright orange with red trimming.

Maker unknown. c. 1860. Velvet, diameter 7"

Nested Blocks

This is a most unusual set of nested blocks which were meant to be educational as well as entertaining. Wild animals are pictured on one side, domestic on the other. The alphabet is here as well as multiplication tables, examples of addition, subtraction, and division, and numbers from 0 to 9; there are scenes of children with pets, some with familiar objects—a little of everything to interest children and encourage them to learn. The blocks were made in the late 1800s when it was the vogue to cram learning into children. An educator looking at this set of blocks would agree that the content is too advanced for the age of the child who would enjoy playing with nested blocks. Nonetheless, this is a beautiful toy.

Maker unknown. Late 1800s. Lithographed paper on wood. When stacked, the 13 blocks stand 57" tall; the smallest block is 4½ x 2", the largest 7½ x 7"

Child with Blocks

This superb oil shows a child holding a column building block with larger cylinders, rectangles, and a cube block on the floor. In order to convey the scale of things in the painting, the artist used several familiar objects—a pencil to the lower left of the child, a button to the right of the child's foot. It is difficult to guess the child's age but, girl or boy, it cannot be more than four years—the right age for simple block building.

The scale of the blocks appears to parallel that of the so-called nursery school, unit, or Caroline Pratt blocks; they are in the same scale as those presently manufactured. Educators endorse blocks of this scale as the most successful toys children will ever have. It is interesting to note that these blocks date from about 1840 or earlier.

Artist unknown. c. 1840. Oil on canvas, 32 x 28"

45

Opposite: **Village Blocks**

One side of the block shows a letter of the alphabet, the other a village building, such as a house, fire department, school, laundry, church, bank. In some ways these blocks resemble village blocks produced in Germany in the 1850s and earlier. This set was found in Pennsylvania, very probably fashioned after the German blocks or done by an immigrant wood-carver. The blocks show some signs of wear, as if they had been played with often.

Folk art. Maker unknown. c. 1900. Wood, 29 blocks from 1¼" to 2" long

Still Banks

Financial success and money were important to parents of the Victorian era. Barter was a thing of the past; people worked by the hour or by the week and were paid in cash. It seemed very important to teach children how to save, to realize the things that money could do; so toy manufacturers made banks in all shapes and sizes, with action (mechanical banks) and without (still).

These particular banks were all produced by George W. Brown. Very similar banks are illustrated in the catalogues of the Merriam Manufacturing Company, Stevens and Brown, Althof, Bergmann, and others. Most tin still banks were made in the shape of buildings. These are complete with Victorian gingerbread.

George W. Brown. 1870s. Tin, from 3¾ x 1¾" to 6 x 5½"

47

Crandall's Building Blocks

Crandall was one of the very few companies that refused to let their products be advertised by a jobber or retailer without using the company name.

These blocks, like most Crandall building toys, came packed in a wooden box built on the same principle of interlocking corners, making a very neat and sturdy package. The instruction sheet gave directions for a few buildings.

Charles M. Crandall. 1867. Wood, blocks in two sizes: 3 x 1¾ x ¼" and 3 x ¾ x ¼"; finials: height 2" and 4"

ABC and Picture Blocks

There are nine blocks here, designed both for play and for learning. They can be set up to form a train on one side and the alphabet in sequential order on the other, with a picture for each letter. Capital letters are printed on the ends of each block. The passengers of the "Cattle" car are animals, dressed in clothing of the day.

Maker unknown. Late 1800s(?). Lithographed paper on wood, 2½ x 2½ x 1"

48

Hill's Alphabet Blocks

These alphabet blocks, among the earliest commercially produced in the United States, are neatly packed in a durable wooden box with sliding cover and a colorful, illustrated label. Each letter is in lowercase on one side of the block and in uppercase on the other. Several sets were made, with variations. Some were lithographed, some painted—on a base coat of paint or directly on the block. Half of this set are red blocks with black letters; the rest are cream-colored with black letters.

S. L. Hill. 1870 (first patented and produced 1858). Wood, painted or lithographed, box: 5¼" square; blocks: 1½" square

Rocking horses, whether one-of-a-kind or manufactured, have existed for centuries. They have always been a satisfactory toy for young children. To have the concept of *horse* brought down to one's own level when one is little opens wide the doors of unlimited travel in imagination.

Bentwood Rocking Horse

This horse was probably commercially produced, but so far there has been no reference found. Its simple design and construction, from eleven pieces of bent wood, is looked at in awe by contemporary toy designers. The beautifully detailed head is carved from one piece of wood. The seat, probably originally made of leather or carpeting, is missing. This toy looks like a piece of contemporary sculpture and demonstrates that good, simple design fits into any period. It is made of reddish-brown stained wood with gold striping.

Maker unknown. Early to mid-1800s. Wood, length 50"; height 16" from the seat to the ground

Packing Crate Rocking Horse

A magnificent horse and pure folk art. The rockers are made from an old packing crate used for a shipment of goods from the United States Bazaar Company, located at 80 Maiden Lane in New York City *(see detail, top)*. The saddle seat is made of a material like oilcloth padded with burlap. The head is carved from one piece of wood, three inches thick. The scroll decoration is in subtle yellows and reds. A very similar design is shown in Marshall and Inez McClintock's *Toys in America* and is attributed to an artisan in Pennsylvania.

Folk art. Maker unknown. Early to mid-1800s. Wood, cloth, and burlap, length 43"; height 12" from the seat to the ground

SYMBOLS OF FREEDOM

Symbols are all around us, from the letters that form the words used here to write about toys to the toys themselves, which symbolize enjoyment, growth, delight at getting a gift, which in turn symbolizes attention from a cherished adult whose approval is so important for the growth and enjoyment of the child who gets the toy. A symbol must be both all-encompassing so as to identify clearly and instantly the thing or idea in question, and capable of quick execution. In the United States the flag is an instantly recognized and highly respected symbol.

Before the Revolution each colony had its own flag. On January 2, 1776, the first United States flag, designer unknown, was raised by George Washington at Cambridge, Massachusetts. Legend has it (the story is still widely told but it has admittedly never been documented) that Washington himself sketched the design of this flag at a meeting held at the home of Betsy Ross, the Philadelphia flag maker. This flag had thirteen alternating red and white stripes with a blue canton (corner square) bearing the crosses of St. Andrew and St. George. Less than six months later the Continental Congress decreed that since church and state had been separated, the canton should show thirteen stars, one for each original state, rather than the two English crosses. This was on June 14, 1776, now designated as Flag Day.

However, in 1791 Vermont was admitted as the fourteenth state, and Kentucky became the fifteenth in 1792. A star and a stripe were added for each one. One of these fifteen-stars-and-stripes flags was flown at Fort McHenry during the War of 1812 while Francis Scott Key was writing "The Star-Spangled Banner."

Center: detail of Historoscope *(see page 79).*

Clockwise from bottom right:

Detail of Tivoli *(see page 64).*

Detail of "Union" boat *(see page 251).*

Detail of Uncle Sam on Velocipede *(see page 71).*

Detail of Drum Dancers *(see page 65).*

Detail of Uncle Sam Bank *(see page 65).*

Eagle Bell Ringer

An illustrated catalogue of the Gong Bell Manufacturing Company for 1900 describes this toy, #50: "Eagle swings and rings bell. Eagle painted in patriotic colors...25 cent size, weight per gross, 150 lbs."

Gong Bell. c. 1900. Cast iron, 4½ x 6"

Eagle Bank

Manufactured in large quantities by the J. and E. Stevens Company, the Eagle Bank is listed in their 1906 catalogue as "#300, 8″ x 6″ x 4″. Packed in a neat wooden box. Retail price $1.00."

The bank was also listed in the 1892 Marshall Field wholesale catalogue at $8.50 per dozen.

J. and E. Stevens. 1883. Cast iron, 6 x 8″

Some representatives must have made projections of the possible future growth of the country and thus the eventual unwieldiness of the flag because in 1818 Congress enacted a new decree, restoring the original thirteen stripes as permanent representation of the thirteen original colonies and states while providing for a star to be added for each new state admitted to the union. This maintained the flag within manageable dimensions. In addition, each state and territory was allowed to have its individual flag as well.

The eagle has been a religious, political, and military symbol throughout the ages, instantly summoning to mind the image of strength and power. If the eagle happens to be the bald eagle, with a wingspread of 5 to 7½ feet, one's political adrenal juices are often tapped. Small wonder that this fiercely protective, independent bird was chosen as the symbol of national strength on the Great Seal of the United States.

Most of us handle this symbol daily on the back of the one-dollar bill. Eagles have been printed on cloth, on paper, on paper money, and on coins made of pottery, copper, nickel, alloys, silver, and gold—the $10 gold eagle and the $20 double eagle—even on wooden nickels and tokens. They have been carved from wood and stone; molded in gutta-percha, celluloid, metal, plastic, and glass; etched in metal for wax seals and in rubber for printing. They have been shown in every conceivable pose, with wings folded, opening, or outspread, or soaring in full majestic flight. Occasionally the eagle has been pictured with a small animal in its claws (but any illustration or story of an eagle snatching anything over seven or eight pounds, such as a three-year-old child, is spurious). They have been depicted on every kind of perch in every possible size; on real and toy drums, banks, bell toys, board games. Step into an antique shop or bid at an auction. If there's an eagle on the object for sale, be prepared to dig a little deeper into your pocket or to up your bid if you're serious about adding the item to your collection.

Banks, both still and mechanical, were devised in order to promote the habit of thrift by making it attractive to children, rewarding—or perhaps consoling—them for giving up their pennies. A mechanical bank that turned out to be quite popular represents an eagle landing on her aerie, which was built just above a fox's den in the Eagle Bank.

However sharp her eye, the eagle is too busy encouraging children to save their coins to see the fox or the fearsome rattler on the other side. When a coin is placed in the eagle's beak, one presses a lever which causes the two eaglets to rise from the nest, mouths agape for food. Just as the mother eagle bends forward to feed them, the coin falls into the nest, bypassing the eaglets, and disappears into the receptacle below. The fox and the rattler—traditionally symbols of danger to man and which here stress the fearlessness of the eagle—watch in safety as the habit of thrift is developed. I wonder how many eagle banks of the day were jammed with crumbs, dropped by sympathetic children who were then often enough sent to bed without supper as a punishment.

The only symbol of peace which I have come across on a toy is the dove with the olive branch, always painted on or attached to the roof of a Noah's Ark. War, however, has always aroused strong feelings of nationalism, which when translated into economics in the United States means "Buy American!" The flag and the eagle left no doubt as to the country of origin of the toy until the Japanese began using these symbols after World War I.

There were other symbols of freedom and patriotism: toy drums have been sold for hundreds of years, symbols of a stirring call-to-arms, symbols of discipline whose steady beat could keep some semblance of order in retreat as well as fire the courage of weary soldiers in the face of danger. That was in the days of hand-to-hand combat. The toy drum is an almost meaningless symbol today.

Often seen in bygone days was Miss Liberty, the feminine figure fashioned after a lesser Greek goddess and revived when the Statue of Liberty was sent to us from France. So far, the women's liberation movement has failed to resurrect her and she is rarely seen today. The Liberty Bell was effective and affective, as were Yankee Doodle and Uncle Sam, the popular masculine symbol which is still in use and which still carries an official connotation. Toys, toy ads, toy catalogues, all have been decorated with these American symbols of freedom. Many toys were made so that a small flag could be inserted into one hand of the figure when the Fourth of July or other parade days rolled around.

There are conflicting stories as to the origin of the name Uncle Sam.

Rocking Eagle Bell Toy

Rocking bell toys are most unusual; very few other figures were used in this manner. The attachment of the bell to the bird is similar to that of the Eagle Bell Ringer (see page 52). The eagle is white underneath and gold on top; the rocker is blue.

Maker unknown. c. 1890. Cast iron, length 4¾"

55

Opposite: **Freedom Bell Ringer**

The tin kneeling figure, hands attached to the bell by a wire, sways back and forth as the toy is pulled. He rings the bell, proclaiming liberty and freedom as the flag waves. What is he celebrating?

Occasionally a slave could buy his freedom, by dint of continuing hard work, service, and exemplary living—like Amos Fortune, the black hero of Jaffrey, New Hampshire. Could he have been celebrating the opening of Tuskegee Institute (1881) or the final passage of the Fifteenth Amendment, guaranteeing him the right to vote? (The fact that the toy is pictured in the Gong Bell catalogue for 1883 does not mean that it had not been made earlier.)

Very few of these toys have turned up; the combination of tin and cast iron, the materials in the Freedom Bell Ringer, was expensive to produce.

Gong Bell. 1880s. Tin and cast iron, 5 x 6"

Ye Hero of 76

Crandall patented the articulated joint in 1867, and had patents issued for this centennial toy in March, May, and October of 1875. As he put it in his advertising: "C. M. Crandall has done it again! has made another splendid thing that will perfectly charm all the LITTLE FOLKS, viz: The Great Centennial Toy." The boast continues, claiming that the hero can be put into "a thousand positions," which may be true—it is a very versatile toy; a flag and a staff are part of the game. Just as current toy makers rallied to the bicentennial theme, so did toy makers one hundred years ago for the centennial.

Charles M. Crandall. 1875. Wood, height 9"

The abbreviation is, of course, short for the United States. The documented story tells of a butcher, one Samuel Wilson of Troy, New York. He and his brother supplied meat for the United States Army during the War of 1812 (sometimes called our Second War of Independence). When Sam also managed to get a job inspecting army supplies, including meat, no one raised the conflict-of-interest issue: Sam Wilson was well-liked and trusted by neighbors, friends, and their children, who called him "Uncle Sam" according to the custom of the times (all adult relatives and close friends were called Uncle, Aunt, or Cousin, never by first name alone). For reasons which he never divulged, or which were never recorded, once the supplies had been inspected and accepted, Sam Wilson stamped them "U.S." The handlers receiving the goods noted the "U.S.," knew they

had been approved, smiled, and called it "Uncle Sam's stamp of approval." Sam Wilson's nickname stuck...and spread. Popular artists and cartoonists of the day picked up the character and there was a proliferation of posters with Uncle Sam urging young men to join the army, urging Americans to sail on American vessels, and urging American housewives to "Buy American!"

I have no idea of Sam Wilson's appearance, but from the beginning, with rare exception, Uncle Sam was portrayed as tall and thin, with white chin whiskers and piercing blue eyes. On one particular toy he stands alone, shorter and stockier than usual, holding an umbrella in one hand; beside him there is a carpetbag, sitting on the platform of the Uncle Sam Bank. When a child puts a coin into Uncle Sam's outstretched hand and touches his arm, Uncle Sam's chin whiskers wiggle, almost as if he were

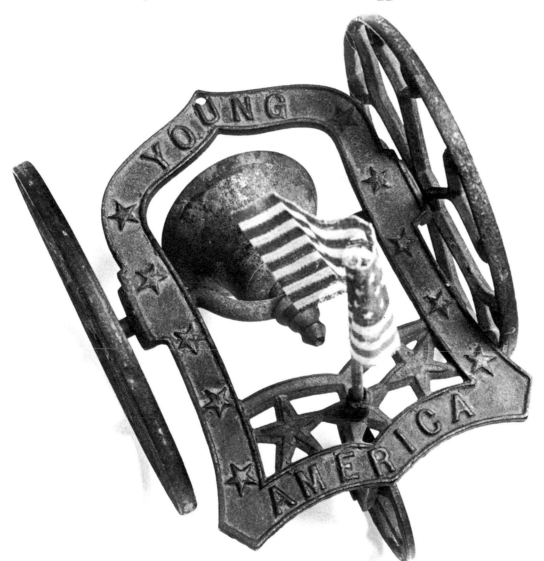

Opposite: **"Independence 1776–1876"**

Produced for the centennial, this toy was designed with as many symbols of freedom as could well be included in one toy: the large bell was reminiscent of the Liberty Bell, the bronze eagle is our national bird, and the flag was made of cloth so that it would wave when the toy was pulled. The dates "1776–1876" are cast in the base.

Gong Bell. 1876. Nickel-plated steel and cloth, length 9½"

Young America Bell Toy

The designer's intent here could only have been to express patriotism: the pull toy is red with a brass bell. The words "Young America" and ten of the thirteen stars are raised and clear, colored in gold on the base; the remaining three stars are red and form a color guard for the flag. It would certainly seem that the designer had the centennial in mind.

The toy is listed in the Gong Bell catalogue of 1878 as part of a line of "Young America Bell Toys"; no others so marked have ever turned up. Other bell ringers of the same and following years were called "Bell Toys" or "Revolving Chimes." In 1878 the toy was #7, indicating that it was one of their earlier toys; in 1880 it was #9; still selling in 1902, it was #12.

Gong Bell used these large (5″) wheels for only two other toys, both revolving chimes. They are different from any found on Gong Bell or any other toys, so here we have one wheel design that so far appears to be exclusive.

Gong Bell. c. 1876. Cast iron and brass, length 7"

Whirligig

This whirligig was made by a most imaginative carver who executed his work with fine detail, though he was obviously an untrained artist. The workmanship and assembly are very good. Wind or no, the flag will always fly, for it is made of tin.

Folk art. Maker unknown. c. 1900. Wood and tin, 6 x 9"

saying "Thank you!" as he drops the coin into his bag. There stands Uncle Sam, on a platform decorated with a colorful eagle, wings outspread—probably the two most often reproduced symbols of freedom and nationalism in this country.

Toy makers also drew many ideas from political events. Famous politicians and military leaders lent their names—sometimes their faces—to particular toys. A major influence on designers was the centennial. There was naturally a great deal of patriotic sentiment in the celebration of the first one hundred years of this nation. Along with all the usual souvenirs attendant on such an auspicious occasion, several toys were designed with patriotic themes. Most carried some centennial motif, and either the word "Centennial" or the dates "1776–1876" somewhere on the toy.

The Columbian Exposition of 1893, held in Chicago, renewed the trend for patriotic toys. The Spanish-American War (1898), the Boxer Rebellion (1900), and the ensuing Open Door policy forced on China kept the trend alive.

Opposite: **North Pole Bank**

The North Pole Bank was produced to celebrate Admiral Robert E. Peary's successful expedition to the North Pole. As was often the case, and still is, designers fashioned toys after the heroes of the day, so this bank and other toys were in mind and even on drawing boards when Peary made his first, highly publicized attempt in 1898 and again in 1905 when he came within 175 miles of the pole. He finally raised the flag on the 90° spot on April 6, 1909, in the company of a servant and three Eskimos.

When a coin is deposited in the slot on the side of the bank, it disappears within the snow pile and the American flag pops out.

J. and E. Stevens. Early 1900s. Cast iron, height 6½"

Front: Horse with Flag

Hull and Stafford. c. 1876. Tin, length 4½"

Rear: Horse with Flag and Wagon

Hull and Stafford. c. 1876. Tin, length 8½"

These two high-spirited horses seem to be heading to a parade—a July Fourth celebration or some other patriotic event. Both horses are white and carry the same flag. The horse alone is mounted on a blue embossed platform with red cast-iron wheels; it is the flag bearer, the leader of the parade. The second horse is pulling a blue open wagon with a red top; the stamping pattern is elegant.

Because of the dates of this early manufacturer and the patriotic colors used, it is fairly safe to say that these toys were some of those redesigned for the centennial, for the same horse and platform exist in other colors, without benefit of flag.

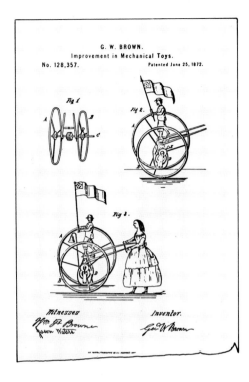

Opposite: Mechanical Hoop with Large Boy and Flag

The patent application for this toy apparently was filed some time after the toy was in production, an oversight that appeared more than a few times among early toy manufacturers. The patent describes a "combination of different diameters of the carrying wheels, the outer hoop measuring 8″ while the inner one measures only 7″." The reason for the new mechanism showed a nice concern for providing satisfying play for children: "as both wheels revolve the same number of times, the larger one moves over the greater distance which causes the toy vehicle to diverge from a straight course and to move in a circle, thus permitting the child to play with the toy without interference of collision with a wall or an enclosure."

This rare and beautiful toy was photographed at the Statue of Liberty in New York Harbor.

George W. Brown. Patented June 25, 1872. Tin, height 10½″

Patriotic Boy Bell Ringer

This is one of the toys that drives researchers and collectors to distraction trying to ascertain the manufacturer. Were all the parts made in one factory? Were they subcontracted or bought outright from other manufacturers? According to billing records, one manufacturer made and sold wheels by the ton every week.

Some collectors identify these wheels as having been used by Althof, Bergmann; the boy appears on toys of other manufacturers. The wheels, the bell, and the tin parts of the toy appear in a Gong Bell catalogue.

This rather elaborate patriotic toy with bell ringing and flags unfurled was photographed at Independence Hall in Philadelphia.

Attributed to Gong Bell. c. 1900. Tin, length 9″

Tivoli

A game resembling bagatelle labeled "Gleason's Tivoli Play," this is an amusing game which can be played by two or more people. Detailed instructions and rules of the game are given on the label. The graphics of the eagle figure and the lithographed designs and colors of the playing board are beautiful.

E. Perry Gleason. c. 1880. Lithographed paper on wood, board 19½ x 10"

64

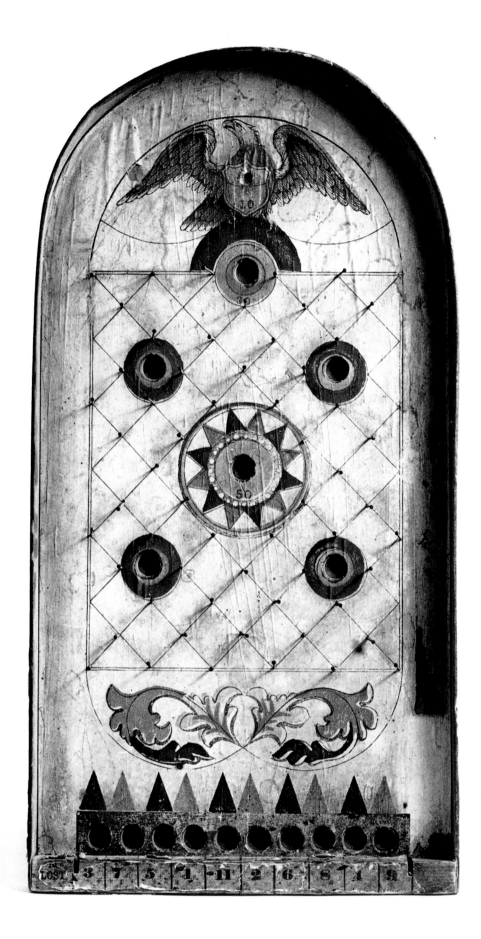

Above: **Uncle Sam Bank**

The coin is placed in Uncle Sam's right hand. When the mechanism is released, the carpetbag opens and the coin drops into the bag.

C. G. Shepard. Patented 1886. Cast iron, height 11½"

Left: **Drum Dancers**

An 1880 dealer's catalogue shows four of this type of toy. The tin drums, decorated with a flying eagle, are stenciled in gold with black lacing; the rims and dancing surface are red. Both figures are made of wood. The man wears a gold shirt and black and red knee pants; the woman wears a yellow dress with red trim.

Ives. 1870s. Wood and tin clockwork toy, height 9½"

Detail of Uncle Sam Bank *(see preceding page).*

Opposite

In the two decades between the International Centennial Exposition of 1876 and the World's Columbian Exposition in 1893, folk art and toys reflected colorful patriotic themes. These three carvings of Uncle Sam and the other Uncle Sam toys were all done during that era. The average toy usually had a longer life one hundred years ago than today, so for the most part the popular ones that had been designed for the centennial were still selling well in the 1890s. They were already the right colors—red, white, and blue— and where the toy had been pulled by one horse it was easy to add another and have a team; to change the flag so as to have the correct number of stars; to add a timely decoration or design.

Left: **Uncle Sam with Flag**

Here is a beautifully carved figure of Uncle Sam, not in the traditional red, white, and blue costume, but in a blue frock coat, the tails of which are studded with painted gray stars; his top hat is gray. He holds a flag in one hand. There appears to be a place for holding an object in the other hand; whatever it might have been, it is missing.

Folk art. Maker unknown; from New Hampshire. Late 1800s. Wood, height 17½"

Center: **Uncle Sam with Flag**

A characteristic rendition of Uncle Sam, he is tall and thin with piercing blue eyes. His clothing borders on the flashy—striped trousers, yellow vest, and red bow tie. He holds a thirteen-star flag in his right hand.

An unusual feature of this folk art carving is that the head is articulated with both a horizontal and a vertical movement, so that in conversation, by tilting Uncle Sam ever so slightly, one could get him to agree or disagree at will.

Folk art. Maker unknown; perhaps from New England. c. 1900. Wood, height 10"

Right: **Uncle Sam Whirligig**

An atypical Uncle Sam, he is short and stocky, and his eyes are black. In spite of his weight, he presents himself as a rigid, military figure in traditional costume. His paddle arms are connected through his shoulders by a piece of metal tubing.

Folk art. Maker unknown; from Millersburg, Pennsylvania. c. 1900. Wood, height 11½", shoulder span 3½"

67

John Bull and Uncle Sam

The Watrous Manufacturing Company of East Hampton, Connecticut, probably made this toy. Watrous and N. N. Hill Brass shared a large factory (the two families were related by marriage). Both companies originally made bells, reins, and small brass hardware. They only added toys to keep the factories going on a year-round basis.

About one hundred years before the Uncle Sam legend came into being in the United States, Great Britain had a similar figure, the now familiar "John Bull." Although he was Queen Anne's court physician and a writer of note, John Arbuthnot is remembered instead for a series of pamphlets he wrote in 1712, humorous criticisms of the Whigs—wealthy merchants and aristocratic landowners. Through the years John Bull and Uncle Sam were used as the subjects of political satire and cartoons to portray the civilized relationship between the two countries, sometimes in a state of cooperation, sometimes in a struggle for power.

This toy is thought to be the original version of one later reissued with two bells, which kept the sparring partners a little further apart.

Watrous. 1890s. Nickel-plated base and cast-iron figures, length 7"

Opposite: **Uncle Sam** and **Columbia**

These figures are part of a group of five sculptures, Andrew Knudsen's signed interpretation of a cult philosophy called "Divine Mathematics." While these toylike designs were made so that all five pieces could be hooked together and drawn along as a pull toy, they nevertheless had some deep religious or philosophical meaning for the maker.

Knudsen used whatever materials were at hand. The aluminum body of Columbia is draped in red and white cloth and a bit of silk flag. Her legs are made of thin-gauge copper; the wig appears to be made from strands of human hair. The handle for pulling the toy is 8″ long. Both ends are looped to enable the attachment of other pieces to either the front or back wheels.

The figure of Uncle Sam is equally interesting. The wheels are shaped from heavy wire; figures of a monkey, an eagle, a devil, and an Indian, tomahawk in hand, ride on the axle. Uncle Sam's body is made of aluminum; his top hat is of tin, trimmed with a bit of flag. His short pants are made from what appears to be a blue tin can; the copper high boots are riveted so that his feet are movable.

Dangling from a delicate chain is a flat timepiece. One side is marked with a *U*, the other with an *S* through which a line has been drawn to indicate a dollar sign ($).

Folk art. Andrew Knudsen. c. 1900. Various materials, height 10″

Uncle Sam on Velocipede

This three-wheeled tin velocipede was fashioned after the velocipede with horse's head made for children from the late 1860s on. When one winds the clockwork, "the figure works the levers in a very easy and natural manner; the toy is propelled either in a straight line or in a large or small circle as desired."

The same velocipede was driven by a clown, a monkey, a boy, or a girl, black or white (see page 179). The girl was the first to be produced, under a patent granted to Nathan Warner of Bridgeport and assigned to the Ives Company for manufacture. Her velocipede is decorated with the head of a horse. The variation "Uncle Sam Going to the World's Fair" (so listed in the Ives catalogue) has an eagle mounted in front. The clockwork mechanism and the action are the same in all the Ives velocipedes.

Ives. c. 1875. Tin and wood, length 9″

Above: **Brass Bell Centennial Top**

This toy in the shape of the Liberty Bell has its crack and the date "1776" etched into it. The underside bears a patent pending date, 1878, maker unknown.

Maker unknown. 1878. Brass, height 2⅞″

Left above: **Folding Paper Hat**

One side of the red, white, and blue folding paper Advertising Hat featured the Republican candidates already mentioned. If that did not suit your political taste, you had only to turn the hat inside out to advertise the Democratic candidates: thirty-six-year-old William Jennings Bryan, and his running mate Arthur Sewall.

This was one of the more exciting campaigns of the day. McKinley did very little campaigning on the road but had great sums of money at his disposal for advertising, including gimmicks such as the top and the hat.

The Boston Sunday Globe. *August 9, 1896. Paper, length 12″*

Wood Spinning Top

This particular top is unusual because of the gold paper band with pictures of the 1896 Republican candidates—William McKinley for president and Garret Hobart for vice-president. Their campaign slogan, "Protection, Sound Money and Prosperity," is also printed. When wound and the center button released, the top spins for quite a while.

Gibbs. 1896. Wood, length 2″

Left: **Suffragette**

She has exactly the same mechanism and motions as the Stump Speaker. She wears a blue-checked dress and bonnet.

Automatic Toy Works. 1875. Wood clockwork toy, height 10"

Right: **Stump Speaker**

"The black man turns his head from side to side, bends forward at the waist, and straightens up. Bangs umbrella on table" to emphasize his point. Whatever his viewpoint, he is patriotic with his red-and-white-checked pants, blue coat, and white-brimmed hat.

Ives. 1882. Wood clockwork toy, height 9½"

Rear: U.S. Capitol

By turning the knobs on either side of the dome, one rolls out a good lesson on the Capitol of the United States—its rooms, building costs, government chambers—and the White House. At the end is a long poem describing each president from Washington to James Garfield, accompanied by portraits.

The toy is so carefully detailed that Reed advertised, "Thousands who have never seen this magnificent structure have here an opportunity, without the expense of a visit." Were this available today, it could be considered a good three-dimensional teaching aid.

W. S. Reed. Patented April 15, 1884.
Lithographed paper on wood, 9½ x 19½"

Elephant Bell Toy and **Mule Bell Toy**

These bell ringers were designed as pull toys. As the wheels turned, a wire activated the animals so that each one swung around and struck the bell. Bases and wheels are the same for both toys. These are only two of a line of animal bell ringers which were very popular at the turn of the century. Whether or not these particular toys were designed with a political viewpoint is not known.

Both toys: Gong Bell. c. 1890s. Cast iron,
length 8"

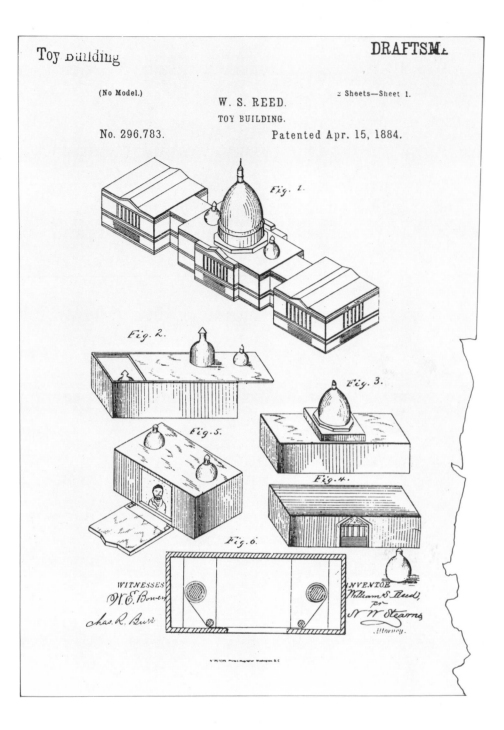

Landing of Columbus

This toy was probably made with the 400th anniversary of the landing of Columbus in mind. Columbus, having sighted land, holds a flag while four oarsmen row him ashore to claim the new land for Spain. The landing craft is an ornate casting of an ancient barge with what looks like a pig for the ship's figurehead. Pigs were considered to bring good luck to children; rattles and teething rings, as late as the beginning of the nineteenth century, had figures of pigs in the design.

Gong Bell. 1892. Cast iron, length 7½″

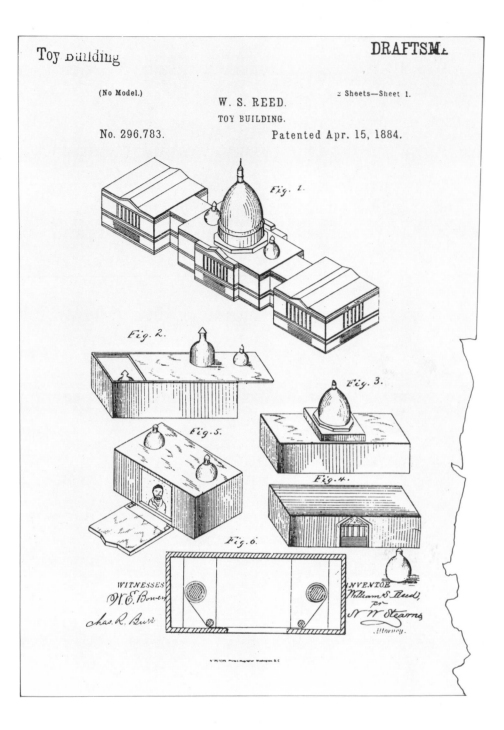

Left: **Historoscope**

The Historoscope was popular for many years; as late as 1892 it still appeared in the wholesale catalogue of a Philadelphia dealer. In an 1860s Bradley catalogue, it was described as "an elegant chromo-lithograph panorama. . . . There is no toy that is more thoroughly appreciated by a little child in the half hour before bed time, as he sits on Mama's or Papa's knee and moves the pictures, meanwhile multiplying eager questions about each one."

Several panoramas were available. This one of George Washington, leading soldiers to battle with sword drawn, has many famous scenes of the Revolutionary War.

Milton Bradley. Undated (designed late 1860s). Lithographed cardboard, 5 x 8"

Right: **George Washington on Horseback**

Except for its ears, the white horse was made from one piece of wood. The reins are leath-er. Washington, in a blue uniform, is 7½" tall; his head and body are carved from one block of wood. The arms are separate and movable. Washington's face is more flat than formed, with a small nose; the perspective is off, but the face is unmistakable. The fat stocky horse looks as if it should be pulling a farm cart rather than carrying the Commander-in-Chief of the United States Army!

Folk art. Maker unknown. c. 1890s. Wood, height 11"

General Grant Smoking a Cigar

When wound, the General raises his arm and puts the cigar holder into a small hole in his mouth. A special toy cigar was available which one could actually light and put in the General's hand, creating the impression that he really was smoking. However, no ashes fell on his gold-braid-trimmed military uniform.

Probably the largest and perhaps the finest automatic clockwork toy made in America, it is much sought after by collectors. Expensive in its time, it was made in smaller quantities than many other toys of its kind, and so is rarely found for sale today. Most automatic clockwork toys produced by Ives or the Automatic Toy Works had smaller bases and figures. General Grant is almost heroic by comparison.

The General's photograph was taken in front of Memorial Hall in Philadelphia, where President Grant spoke during the Centennial Exposition.

Ives. c. 1876. Clockwork toy, height 14"

Opposite: **Oliver Hazard Perry Whirligig**

Oliver Hazard Perry was a hero of the War of 1812. His victory over the British gave the United States control of Lake Erie. His succinct report, "We have met the enemy and they are ours," was instantly famous and has often been repeated.

The carving was found in Rhode Island, where Oliver Hazard Perry was born.

Folk art. Maker unknown. c. 1850. Wood, height 30½"; paddles: length 25"

Soldiers' Drill

Although stationary, these four soldiers are so well carved that they give the impression of being in a parade or drill. The soldiers are mounted on a wooden base; their rifles are disproportionately large—6″ long.

Folk art. Maker unknown. c. 1900. Wood, 5½ x 16 x 6″

"The Chinese Must Go"

"The Chinese Must Go" was a familiar cry in the late 1870s. From 1850 on, Chinese laborers flooded into California; their cheap labor was welcomed in building the first transcontinental railroad. By the time it was finished, times were getting hard; many of the 1850s pioneers were looking for work, but Chinese labor was cheaper. Toward the end of the 1870s there were anti-Chinese riots in California. The antagonism and political dealings resulted in the Chinese Exclusion Act, vetoed in 1879 but passed in 1882; it excluded Chinese laborers from the United States for a decade. The cap pistol represents one "Chinaman" trying to escape the immigration officer who grasps the Oriental's pigtail.

The Oriental and one leg of his captor are stationary parts of the casting. The official's other leg is attached by a spring so that as the trigger is pulled, the official's free leg is cocked for action. The cap is placed in the mouth of the "Chinaman." When the trigger is pulled, the official kicks the "Chinaman," causing his mouth to shut and exploding the cap.

Ives. Patented 1879. Cast iron, length 4¾"

"Uncle Sam Says 'Git!'"

The Spanish General Valeriano Weyler y Nicolau had a long and unsavory history of cruelty and oppression in the Philippines (1888) and later in Cuba (1896). As a result of official American protests, he was recalled to Spain in 1897.

A cap is placed in the end of General Weyler's coattail; when Uncle Sam kicks him out of Cuba, the cap explodes.

Maker unknown. 1890s. Cast iron, length 5"

General Butler

This Ives rendition of General Benjamin Franklin Butler is based on a specially patented device resembling a roller skate in the soles of the shoes. According to Ives's publicity, the figures could "walk quite a distance when wound—from 20 to 30 feet, in good imitation of life." Ives made other walking figures, Santa Claus (see page 151) and Uncle Tom among them, all illustrated in an undated catalogue c. 1893. Santa Claus was the most expensive, wholesaling at $33 per dozen, while the others all sold for $30. General Butler (1818–1893), one of the less successful Civil War Union generals, was originally a Democrat, served in Congress as a Republican ("Rabid Republican" is what his peers called him), then as a Greenbacker (an advocate of currency expansion), and in 1884 was a presidential nominee of the Greenbackers and independent Democrats. A highly controversial but famous New England figure, he was a "natural" as the subject of an Ives walking toy.

Ives. 1880s. Cast iron and wood clockwork toy, height 10"

85

Above: **Boy Pulling Roundabout**

This toy presents a problem and a challenge: Who designed it? Who manufactured it? The toy is japanned; that and other small details make one say, "Fallows!" But one figure so strongly resembles a George Brown figure that one would venture that it *is* one. Could it be a replacement? The base is Fallows green, yet it looks as if it might originally have been tricolored—green, white, and russet (but the russet might be traces of rust). The undercarriage is red.

Maker unknown. c. 1870s. Tin, 7 x 7"

Below: **Young Recruit**

The Young Recruit has the same semi-mechanical motion as the other Fallows patented toys. The horse and rider here were also used in the Jerome Park toy on page 124. Except for his knapsack, the boy is the same as other Fallows figures. It appears that originally the toy had three other soldiers. Although only partially complete, it is such an unusual toy that it has an important place in the collection.

The soldier is dressed in a red uniform striped in black and is wearing black leggings or boots.

Fallows. 1880s. Tin, base: length 9"; soldier: height 2¾"

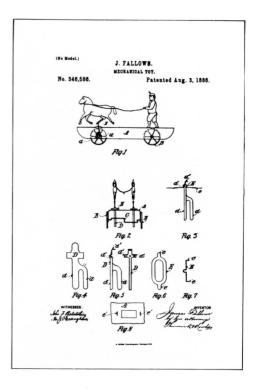

Revolving Parade Pull Toy

The soldiers, marching and on horse-back, are mounted on an unusual circular platform. When pulled, a specially designed wheel under the platform causes it to revolve. The figure in the center on a raised platform, apparently the leader of the group, has his hat in hand to salute the spectators along the line of march.

Attributed to Hull and Stafford. c. 1870s. Tin, platform: diameter 9"; soldiers: height 2½" and 2"

Military Tenpins

The ten soldiers wear identical uniforms except for color: five have red jackets and blue trousers, the other five have blue jackets and red trousers. Hats and trousers are painted; the jackets and facial features are lithographed in meticulous detail.

While some submit that this set is of European origin, the original box and label appear to be American. These soldiers have a regal Prussian manner; the object of the game was to roll the ball and knock over as many of the "enemy" as possible.

Maker unknown. Patented May 5, 1885. Painted and lithographed wood, height 10"

Opposite: **Soldiers on Wheels**

The only toy maker showing three-dimensional soldiers on wheels in a catalogue was Althof, Bergmann. These have different uniforms, but the catalogue illustration is hand drawn.

Attributed to Althof, Bergmann. c. 1875. Tin, height 3½"

The drum in the background is not a toy. Made by G. and F. Boistmann and Company in the Civil War period, it is marked on the rim: Mike Cochran—The Gallant Braves—the 69—Irish Volunteers. It is 16" high and 54" in diameter. Except for the lacings, which have been replaced, it is in its original condition.

Automated Sand Toy

The front is closed in with glass; the mechanism is delicate and often comes apart. When the box is turned counter-clockwise several times, the sand trickles over the wheel and activates the figures. Lincoln is cranking the hurdy-gurdy while the monkey, thought to represent Gideon Welles, Lincoln's Secretary of the Navy and his staunch supporter, is playing the violin.

    The directions on the label are legible but the name of the manufacturer is not. It is believed to be Gerrard Calgani or Cargani of Hartford, Connecticut.

Gerrard Calgani or Cargani. 1860s. Cardboard and glass, 10 x 8 x 2¾"

"Monitor"

The "Monitor" is featured in the George Brown Sketchbook of 1870 in the exact colors and size of this toy, complete with revolving turret. However, it will never sink as it is a wheeled pull toy.

Having saved the Union Navy from the *Virginia* (the *Merrimac*, repaired and renamed) in the celebrated battle between the two ironclads, the *Monitor* came to an inglorious end: she sank while being towed to port during a storm on New Year's Eve, 1862. Lost on the bottom of the sea for years, she was spotted by sonar south southeast of Cape Hatteras in 1974, and a ship's lantern was retrieved. The spot was designated a Marine Sanctuary under government protection.

George W. Brown. 1870. Tin, length 14"

Opposite: General Jackson Side-Wheeler

So few toys were labeled a hundred years ago, and of those, naturally, the paper labels could hardly be expected to survive. Yet here is a clockwork tin side-wheeler bearing the original label of George W. Brown! It appears in the George Brown Sketchbook (1870), under the name "Crescent" ("14½" long   6" high #5, per doz. $21.00"), as well as in the 1872 Stevens and Brown catalogue. A smaller version ("7 in. long . . . 3 in. high   #6 . . . per doz. $9.00") was put out under the names "Victory" and "Niagara."

Stonewall Jackson was a Confederate general held in great esteem and affection by his men, by whose fire he was mistakenly shot and mortally wounded after the Battle of Chancellorsville. It is possible that the "General Jackson" is an earlier model, or one intended for sale in the South.

George W. Brown. 1870. Tin clockwork toy, length 14½"

Taylor Boat

The tin boat photographed here is probably one of the earliest toys commercially made in the United States. It was named for General Zachary Taylor, who earned wide renown for his victory at Buena Vista in 1847. He was outspoken in his support of the Wilmot Proviso—no slavery, whatever the latitude, in territory gained from the war with Mexico. Elected on the Whig ticket in 1849, he had a very short presidency, dying of cholera a year later. Francis, Field and Francis later pro-duced a train and an omnibus named after Taylor. Old "Rough and Ready," as he was nicknamed by his troops, was also popular in the toy world at mid-century.

Francis, Field and Francis. 1840s. Tin, length 9½″

Opposite: **Pull for the Shore**

The pictures on the boat are of a plantation manor house and two smaller houses for slaves and, on the bow of the boat, a levee with tall stacks of baled cotton and boats coming into a busy harbor.

The black men in the boat appear smiling and happy. As the toy is pulled, the man in the bow plays the cymbals while the man in the stern rings a bell; the men in the middle sing and "truck" to the music.

W. S. Reed. Patented 1881. Lithographed paper on wood, length 17″

President's Private Car

This red car is part of the Ives "Excursion
Train," which measures 28″ long including
the locomotive and tender. Most early cast-
iron trains were made without passengers; the
"President" car has sixteen—attired in bright
red, silver, and gold clothing—all an integral
part of the casting. The car was molded in
two halves and joined together in a second
operation.

Ives. Patented 1895. Cast iron, length 12″

FAMILIAR ANIMALS

Current studies in nursery, kindergarten, and primary schools show that up to eight or nine years of age, children maintain the strongest interest in familiar animals as subjects of favorite stories.

When a wide-eyed child asks about how Mother Raccoon dealt with her willful child, one has to know one's child and the situation in order to respond to his real question: is he sounding you out as to how he is going to be dealt with in a similar situation; is he trying to see whether he can trust you for help; or is he asking for simple, factual information? It is easier for him to use the animal as the vehicle for gathering his information.

Familiar animals are part of known territory, usually a relatively safe environment whose surprises one can deal with, even at three or four years of age. True, the circle of familiar animals used to be much wider. Today it is fairly well limited to a dog, a cat, or some goldfish; according to the home or school, a guinea pig, gerbil, or rabbit may occasionally be part of the scene. The ties between children and animals have been fairly well broken except for those who live near a children's zoo, in remote country, or in farming areas. The days of Mr. McGregor and Peter Rabbit are gone.

Because both children and adults have always been interested in animals, every toy designer and manufacturer included them in a variety of toys, either alone or in combination with other figures.

Three-Wheeled Walking Horse

A beautifully designed walking horse, it captures the feeling of folk art more than any other manufactured toy. Ives also manufactured this horse as a conventional four-wheeler. Since only one three-wheeler has come to light, it is not known if the company experimented with just one three-wheeled model, either producing it in very limited quantity or deciding not to produce it at all, limiting themselves to the sturdier four-wheeled model.

Ives. Late 1800s. Cast iron, length 7"

99

Wiggly Dog

The body of the dog is in nine sections, including the head and tail. It was made in the 1890s by an unknown Pennsylvania folk artist, who probably got the idea from the wiggling snakes and alligators mass-produced for generations. The dog is fairly realistic but woeful-looking. Its construction is fragile: a thin tape glued to the sections of its body holds it together. It is cleverly mounted on tiny wheels, one in each paw, so that it can be pulled, gently.

Folk art. Maker unknown. 1890s. Wood, length 12½"

Shepherd and Dog

One of the larger tin toys attributed to Althof, Bergmann, it is believed to have been produced for only a short time because of its high production costs. The shepherd is dressed in blue with red boots and hat; the brown dog carries a yellow basket. The only known illustration of this toy (#89), in an Oscar Strassburger jobber's catalogue (New York, 1880), indicates that there are *two* sheep and a ram and *two* goats as well as the other figures, so that one goat appears to be missing here.

Attributed to Althof, Bergmann. c. 1874. Tin, length 13"; height: shepherd, 6"; farm animals, 3¾"; dog, 2½"

Girl Platform Toy

The little girl is beautifully dressed in a cream-colored jacket, bright blue skirt, red shoes, stockings, and cap. The black goat with gray ears and whiskers sports a blue saddle or saddle blanket trimmed in red; its bridle is golden. The lamb is white; its bell is red. In spite of the distorted scale this is a most attractive pull toy.

Attributed to Hull and Stafford. 1880s. Tin, base: length 9"; goat: 6 x 5½"; girl: height 3½"

101

Balancing Horses

Balancing toys produced in America were copied designs of European toys made long before the settling of the colonies here. An analysis of the wood, paint, and construction of the wooden folk art toy indicates that it was made in about the same period as the manufactured tin toy.

According to the manufacturer's catalogue, the tin toy (right) was produced in three sizes of which this is the largest. The folk art wooden toy (left), of course, is one of a kind.

The carver's skill is evident in the detail and proportions. The weighting and positioning of the ball were so precise that a college professor used the toy to demonstrate the principle of balance to a physics class.

Tin Horse

Hull and Stafford. 1870s. Tin, height 15"; base: length 9"

Wooden Horse

Maker unknown. c. 1870s. Wood, height 10¾"; base: length 5½"

Opposite: Man with Cigar on Horseback

The whimsical Man with Cigar was found in Pennsylvania. Head and body are carved from one piece of wood; hat, legs, arms, and the legs of the horse are all glued and nailed on. The rider has black britches, red coat and legs; his hat is black with a silver band.

Folk art. Maker unknown. c. 1900. Wood, length 7"

Opposite: **Horse on Sculptured Base**

All that is known about the inventor, William A. Harwood of Brooklyn, is that over a period of five or six years he had several patents for toys. This patent application was filed April 25, 1876, for: "A toy horse, whereof the horse figure proper is mounted on and connected to the axles of the wheels by coiled, arched, or otherwise elevated platform or support. . . ." The curved platform provided a stronger mount, on a narrower base, using less metal. "By mounting it higher, the horse of a given size looks larger, and makes a more attractive toy."

This horse, one of the most graceful of all American tin toys, was photographed in a wooded area near Philadelphia.

Merriam. 1876. Tin, length 8½"

Rabbit

Rabbit figures are rare among old tin toys. Some collectors have attributed the toy to George Brown, who produced a varied line of animal toys this size. So far as we know, there is no documentation for this assumption.

Maker unknown. Tin, length 3"

Boy with Whip

The Boy with Whip is about as tall as the rabbit is long. They make a colorful pair, photographed appropriately enough at the well-known businessmen's luncheon club in Philadelphia called "The Rabbit."

Althof, Bergmann(?). c. 1874. Tin, height 3½"

Right: **Rocking Bell Toy**

A beautiful bell toy, with figures resembling ones used by Althof, Bergmann.

Attributed to Althof, Bergmann. c. 1880. Tin, length 7"

Below

Left: **Parrot on Wheels**

The whole toy is very colorful: the parrot has red, green, blue, and yellow "feathers." As the toy is pulled, the parrot rocks back and forth. The weighted metal base, popular on a number of George Brown toys, keeps the parrot upright at all times.

George W. Brown. 1870s. Tin, height 3"

Right: **The Girl in Fairy Coach**

The Girl in Fairy Coach is definitely a George Brown figure but the wheels are unlike those on any other Brown toy. No documentation of any kind has ever been found on this toy; nothing is known of the designer who drew this fantasy of a coach made of leaves.

Attributed to George W. Brown. 1870s. Tin, length 6"

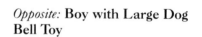

Opposite: **Boy with Large Dog Bell Toy**

One of the most unusual larger-scale bell toys, when it is pulled, or pushed, the dog's orange platform rocks back and forth, producing a pretty jingling sound of the large and small bells. The boy, dressed in blue, is dwarfed by the brown-and-white dog. Some nineteenth-century designers must have taken pleasure in distorting the scale; quite a few such toys were produced.

Althof, Bergmann. 1880s. Tin, overall length 11"; base: length 9¾"; dog: 5¾ x 7¼"; boy: height 3½"

Overleaf: **Hoop Race**

Animals in rolling hoops were very popular. They were part of the standard line of such companies as Fallows, Althof, Bergmann, Merriam, and George Brown. The Rabbit-in-Hoop (left) was made by Merriam and is considered among the rarest today.

The horse in the medium-sized hoop second from the left (maker unknown) is unusual. Although made of two pieces of tin, it is flat when compared to any other tin horse. The hoop itself, of corrugated tin, is also different from the others. The other horses-in-hoops are attributed to George Brown (third from the left) and Althof, Bergmann (second from the right).

The Dog-in-Hoop (front, right) was illustrated in the Stevens and Brown catalogue of 1872 and sold for "$13.50 per gross at wholesale."

The Boy-with-Hoop (right) is marked on the outer side of the wheel: "Chime pat. Aug. 20 and 27, 1872," and, below it: "May 19, 1874   Hoop and Boy   patent applied for." It appears that the original toy, called "The Chime," was just a rolling hoop with a bell. When the boy was added a new patent application was necessary to protect the model. Educated guessing attributes this toy to Stevens and Brown, whose catalogues featured many hoop toys.

Various tin toy manufacturers.
c. 1870s. Diameter from 4½" to 9"

107

Alligator and Boy Bell Toy

The bronze-colored alligator rests on a silver log; the black boy has painted blue jacket, red trousers, and yellow hat. "The movement of the toy bounces the boy and rings the gong."

N. N. Hill Brass. c. 1900. Cast iron, 5 x 6"

Camel Bell Toy

The yellow camel is mounted on a green base. The off-center large wheels in front give the toy a bobbing motion when pulled. The boy rider holds a swagger stick to prod the camel; the saddlebags are ornate and colorful.

Attributed to Althof, Bergmann. 1874. Tin, length 9", height 7" from base to top of bell

The thirteen tin animals were made by various tin toy makers—among them, several by George Brown, and by Hull and Stafford, Althof, Bergmann, and Merriam—from the 1860s to the 1880s. They are from 2¼″ to 4½″ long, from 2″ to 4″ high, and are all about 2″ wide. Most of them cost about three cents apiece wholesale, so they were among the most available toys of the day.

Carved Wood Horses

The two beautifully carved horses on the right and left were found in Maine. At first glance the middle horse seems to be the work of the same person. However, on examination the horse is found to be much lighter as the wood is considerably older than that of the other two. Subtle differences in the carving techniques have convinced us that it was done by different hands. It was found in Connecticut.

Folk art. Makers unknown. c. 1880s. Wood, horses on right and left: length 9''; horse in center: length 8''

Opposite: All three of these folk toys have been so expertly executed that they look almost machine-made.

Left: The peacock has traces of old blue paint with some yellow dots (representing eye spots) on the tail. The body is mounted on a nail.

Folk art. Maker unknown; from Pennsylvania. c. 1880s. Painted wood, 5¼ x 3¾''

Center: The greyhound really looks de-

jected—tail between its legs, ears drooping, and a soulful expression on its face.

Folk art. Maker unknown; probably from Ohio. c. 1900. Painted wood, length 5½''

Right: An extraordinary carving—the Dalmatian is standing at attention, tail erect, and seems to have its gaze fixed on a particular person or object.

Folk art. Maker unknown; from Ohio. c. 1900. Painted wood, length 5''

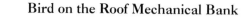

Bird on the Roof Mechanical Bank

The coin slot is in the comb of the bird, perched on the roof of a church. As the lever is released, the bird moves forward, leans over the chimney, and deposits the coin. Although this bank is manufactured, it has the look of a piece of folk art; the detail of the casting, the open window pattern, the grace of the bird all combine to make it a most attractive toy.

J. and E. Stevens. Patented March 5, 1878. Cast iron, length 4½"

Above: **Cat Animated Cap Pistol**

The paw in which the cap is placed is an integral part of the casting; the gun is cocked by lifting the other paw, which comes down and explodes the cap when the trigger is pulled. The cat's tail is molded to form the handle.

Maker unknown. c. 1882. Cast iron with a japanned bronze finish, length 5"

Left: **Monkey Churning**

The monkey has a wooden body, metal feet, and a composition head. Its velvet knee breeches are trimmed with gold tinsel ribbon; the silk waistcoat is trimmed with lace. Its legs and arms are made of a plush material, sometimes called mohair—one of the first uses of plush by an American toy maker to cover an animal. Instructions say to wind the clockwork and watch "the monkey churn vigorously." The wholesale price was $30 per dozen, each packed in its own box.

Ives. Patented March 31, 1874. Iron and wood clockwork toy, height 11½"

117

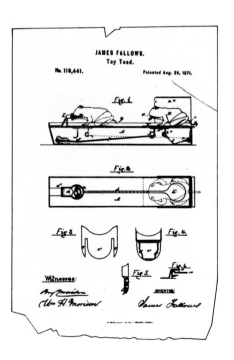

Toy Toad

There is some controversy as to whether the Toad was produced as a toy or as a bank. From the collector's point of view, it is unimportant because it is such a delightful piece. This particular toad is the actual patent model submitted by Fallows to the Patent Office. Its original tags indicate that it was received in the Patent Office on June 29, registered on July 6, and patented August 29, 1871, No. 118,441.

In his *A Handbook of Old Mechanical Penny Banks* (1948), John Meyer describes the toy as follows: "Frog in Den—Tin. The den, or well with cover, is about 8″ high and 10″ long. Place the frog in the den, close the lid, put a coin on the holder opposite the den. Take the cover off: the frog jumps out, moves forward and grabs the coin." The patent model shown here is a little smaller than the dimensions of the toy listed above, but the mechanism is the same.

Fallows. Patented August 29, 1871. Tin, overall length 9½″; toad: length 2½″

Opposite: Squeak Toys

Squeak toys originated in Europe but many were made in the United States, particularly in Pennsylvania. They were extremely popular in the late 1800s and came in a wide variety of characters and sizes. The figures are usually mounted on wooden bases and then attached to a bellows made of leather or cloth. When pressed together, the bellows makes a small squeak. Often the birds or other fowl have coiled spring wires for legs, so when the bellows is squeezed, they bob about. Some squeak toys, such as the dog, have tiny wheels. These are really only for effect since most of them will not move.

The five figures here, makers unknown, are made of papier-mâché, the bellows of wood and cloth or leather. They range from the 4½″-high cat to the 8½″-high rooster.

RACE AND CHASE

The chase and the hunt—the oldest and most primitive method of obtaining food sustained man's first existence, gave him meat to eat and skins to protect him from the elements. As man settled in permanent habitats and began to grow much of his food supply, the chase gradually took less time, developed a social side, and became a sport with an element of chance to make it more exciting.

In an 1852 Philadelphia publication, *Little Charley's Games and Sports*, we are told that Charley's "little brother Willie has just got into jacket and trousers, and he rides on a stick-horse all about the yard." Charley indulged in "hoop trundling—always healthful and invigorating and developes the muscles and the limbs." The author further comments, "The girls have lately taken up trundling the hoop; and I think it very proper they should do so, for the exercise is quite as necessary and as suitable for them as for the boys." And on another day Charley and some friends set out for a combination picnic and berry-picking project, "unless they happen to espy a wood chuck or a squirrel. In that case, as Charley's dog, Rover, is to go along with them, I am afraid they will try the sports of the chase."

In *Play of Man* (1901) Karl Groos writes, "The impulse to pursue a fleeing creature, or to flee and hide from approaching danger is as much an inborn instinct in man as in animals." Thus, hide-and-seek, tag, games like Capture the Flag and Red Rover are played in some form by children all over the world. The magic feeling of sharing their fun as a group adds

Hunter on Horse

The horse, rust color with black markings, is mounted on a piece of spring steel; when this is pressed down and released the horse bobs up and down in a diminishing gallop. The rider, dressed in a long red hunting coat and cap, brown trousers and boots, is attached with a pin and moves forward and back in rhythm with the horse.

The detail of workmanship is so precise that it could well have been made in a factory. Yet, so different from any other toy seen, it is unique and would seem to have been made by one person for a particular child. This is the kind of toy that is difficult to place. Our feeling is to consider it an extremely well-designed and -executed folk art toy.

Maker unknown. c. 1890. Wooden horse on spring, length 12"

121

to their pleasure. Based on instinct but played according to rules, this kind of play has a built-in permanence and remains popular forever. Dogs chase cats, cats chase birds, and children chase each other, all usually for the sheer fun of pursuit. Laughing and screaming in half-real, half-pretend fear, children automatically run when chased by other children, who, when they *do* catch their quarry amid peals of laughter, race off on another chase, until energy is gone and the chase perforce comes to an end. Being chased can be a way of living through some of the terrors of childhood out in the open. In the child's own world, under rules that have been agreed upon in advance, the child can race, chase, and be chased in safety.

Animals and humans came together in the chase when the wily fox fled the hounds of the rich who followed in pursuit; riding to hounds was a favorite sport among the gentry in England, who introduced it into the southern colonies where there was far more social life than in New England. Poor southern farmers ran foxes at night, following their hounds on foot. According to one historian, they carried a jug of home brew or mountain dew to liven up the proceedings.

From the chase was developed another popular sport: a pig or a goose was greased; players, on foot or on horseback, chased the greased animal and tried to grab it and hold it. This was lively sport throughout the colonies. Once man was able to purchase food, although he still opted for the chase it was more hunting for sport—with bow and arrow or gun, usually under set rules or laws.

Horse racing was widespread in America from revolutionary days on. One post–Civil War horse, Dexter, broke the record for the miler and the trotter, and added a new record for pulling a wagon over a one-mile course. Dexter was a great favorite with the public. He was described as an unbelievably long-legged brown horse with four white feet, a white blaze, and piercing eyes, not only fast but beautiful and intelligent. It is not surprising that such a horse, with his jockey and colors, sulky, wagon, and stables, should have been the subject of toys. They were produced in quantity by several of the well-known toy companies of the era. All toy makers produced toys drawn by horses.

Many mothers and nannies put a cotton-tape harness on their charges, originally meant to prevent them from falling and later to keep

A race for all time—for all creatures, great and small, made by various tin toy makers, including Fallows, Althof, Bergmann, and possibly Hull and Stafford, probably between 1870, or a bit earlier, and the end of the century. They range in size from the largest, the Dog with Jockey on the extreme left—11″ high and 13″ long—to the smallest, the Horse with Jockey (front, center)—4¼″ high and 6½″ long.

Jerome Park

The Jerome Park racetrack in the Bronx, then an outlying country district of New York City, was built by the father of Jenny Jerome, American mother of the great English statesman Sir Winston Churchill.

The jockeys on horses rock back and forth independently, each in his own rhythm (a special Fallows patent), which seems to make for more vivid action and to give the impression of a race. This base is japanned in blue; the jockeys appear to be from the same stable, all sporting the same colors—red waistcoats and white jodhpurs.

Fallows. c. 1880. Tin, length 8"

124

Opposite: Race Course Bank

Stevens and Brown listed this mechanical bank in their 1872 catalogue as the Race Course Bank. Collectors usually refer to it as the Horse Race Bank. The bank structure is of cast iron; the horses and riders are made of tin. A spring top must be wound on a string before the bank will operate. Dropping a coin in the opening starts the race. When the spring winds down, the horse nearest the post is the winner.

Stevens and Brown. 1872. Cast iron and tin, diameter 6", height 5¼"

Front: Dexter

Here he is—the champ! A winner for sure: rich brown coat, black mane and tail. Red jacket, yellow jodhpurs with a black side stripe, and black boots, seated on a green sulky, the jockey is almost as elegant as his mount. This toy version of Dexter, the famous nineteenth-century thoroughbred, is winning the race.

Note that the mechanism is skillfully enclosed, attached to the rear left hoof, making the gig realistic as well as artistic. The toy sold wholesale for $12 per dozen.

Stevens and Brown. c. 1870. Tin, length 15"

Rear: White Horse Gig

The white ringer for Dexter was manufactured by the same company at about the same time. This gig is also green with bright red braces; the jockey wears an almost identical outfit. A wheel attached to the horse's left front and hind legs enables the toy to turn in the desired direction. These toys have excitement built in, the excitement that trotting races still bring to their fans.

Stevens and Brown. c. 1870. Tin, length 13½"

125

them from running too far off. Small bells on the reins jingled and made it somewhat of a game: children played at horse-and-driver. The rules of the game were modeled on the way Papa dealt with the family horse. It was fairly acceptable indoor play, until the "horse" tired of his orderly procession through the house and threw over the traces.

There are also board games like Parcheesi and Chutes and Ladders in which the race and the chase element lends an alluring quality to what would otherwise be a fairly dull procedure: rolling dice and moving playing pieces accordingly. Most hunting among toy figures is done at point-blank with a gun, as in the Buffalo Bill pull toy, or in the form of the chase, as in many bell toys, an endless pursuit in which the quarry is never caught.

Rocking Horse Race

Here is a race to charm the eye, to stir a sense of rhythm, and to make one smile from love of rocking horses. The entries include two Fallows horses on deep rockers (extreme left and right), one Hull and Stafford which stands on a metal rod rather than being suspended from the ends of the rockers (second from left). The other two horses, on wire rockers, remain unidentified, although the upper horse resembles very closely the horse on page 128 which is riding with the greyhound. These are all tin toys.

The large Fallows horse measures 6 x 7" and the small one 3¾ x 4¼". The Hull and Stafford horse is 4½ x 6¼". The large unidentified steed measures 5 x 6", while the small one is 3¼ x 3½". All were produced in the 1870s.

Horse and Rider

The man is riding, presumably to the hunt, in a blue rather than a red coat, but his white trousers have a red stripe. The greyhound, wearing a red collar, is unusual as a hunting dog.

Hull and Stafford. c. 1870. Tin, length 8½"

Oarsmen

Rowing, popular in England, became an official intercollegiate sport in the United States with the 1852 regatta between Yale and Harvard. Both rowing and sculling have been Olympic Games events since 1900; they are still popular college and club sports.

The top toy would properly be called a rowing toy since it is manned by eight oarsmen; sculling teams have one, two, or four oarsmen; rowing teams have two, four, or eight oarsmen, with or without a coxswain.

When pulled, or pushed, the oarsmen in these cast-iron sculls row in unison. The top and bottom boats are tan with green bottoms; the middle boat is all red with yellow wheels.

Top: *U.S. Hardware. 1890s. Cast iron, length 14"*

Center: *Wilkins. 1890s. Cast iron, length 10½"*

Bottom: *U.S. Hardware. 1890s. Cast iron, length 9"*

Team Riders

The black team riders are on a delicate base painted an attractive orange-red. The wheels have heart-shaped spokes. The slightly off-center axle gives the horses in motion a satisfying galloping effect.

Wilkins. 1890s. Cast iron, length 7"

Horse with Rider

The 1895 Wilkins toy catalogue shows this single horse with rider bell toy. Both horse and rider are painted a dramatic black, while the wheels, with their unique star-shaped spokes, and frame are red.

Wilkins. 1890s. Cast iron, length 6¼"

Buffalo Bill

Here is a pull toy of the historical figure Buffalo Bill. Though dressed like Robin Hood in a green hunting outfit with a red cap, he is mounted on a white steed and portrayed hunting buffalo for the workers in the railroad construction camps. William Cody, his real name, gave up hunting buffalo by the time he was thirty and went into show business. His Wild West Show traveled all through the United States and Europe. A popular hero, he was a "natural" for an action toy figure.

The buffalo are a realistic brown with black manes; all the figures are mounted on the familiar green base with gold stripes.

Fallows. c. 1880s. Tin, length 8¾″

131

All the toys on this page and the page opposite, as well as the Buffalo Bill toy on page 131 and the Jerome Park toy on page 124, are from a series of movable combination toys made by James Fallows of Philadelphia. All have sides that cover the mechanism and wheels of the same design.

Girl with Ducks and Chicks

The chicks are activated by a concentric rod attached to the wheels. When the toy is pulled the chicks go distractedly back and forth in a continuing chase to keep up with the ducks and the girl.

The baby chicks are white, the ducks are white with yellow beaks, the girl's dress is white with red trim, and her hat is yellow. They are set in a Fallows green base.

Fallows. c. 1880s. Tin, length 8"

Girl with Swans

As the toy is pulled the swans run from the girl. They are perfectly safe, for the girl is stationary. The girl's dress is yellow with white trim; she is on a green base.

Fallows. Patented 1886. Tin, length 8"

Boy Chasing Pigs

The man and boy chasing a pair of pigs makes an amusing pull toy with more action than some of the others in Fallows's series of movable combination toys. The outsize pigs, which appear to be of the Brown Spotted Swine variety, popular at the time, seem to be enjoying the chase. The man is dressed in a red jacket, green trousers, and black cap. The boy wears a blue waistcoat and white trousers. The base is again Fallows green, with gold stripes.

Fallows. c. 1880. Tin, length 8¾"

Dog Chasing Rabbits

This chase seems to be a really hot pursuit with the dog close on the heels of the rabbits. But the poor canine is panting while the rabbits look quite fresh and appear to be running with less effort. The dog is solid brown; he wears a red collar. The rabbits are gray with brown spots, rather an unusual species. The pull toy has a green base.

Fallows. c. 1880s. Tin, length 8¾"

133

Dog and Cat Bell Toy

A black-and-white cat baits the brown-spotted white dog from a safe distance. As the toy is pulled across the floor the dog rushes out of its splendiferous doghouse with red and gold cathedral windows and a yellow roof, but the cat always retreats in time. This toy also has a green base.

Gong Bell. 1872. Cast iron, length 9"

Boy and Hog

As the motor unwinds and the toy moves along the floor, the hog is activated by the wire attached in front. The up and down movement of the hog causes the boy, holding the hog's tail, to move upward and forward. This quarry looks as if it has been caught, but so long as the boy holds only the tail, the chase is not over. The boy wears yellow trousers and cap and a red shirt.

George W. Brown. 1870. Tin clockwork toy, length 5"

Four Equestrians

Here are four horses obviously relishing both the pace and the chase. The men wear red coats and hats and tan jodhpurs. Two of the riders are fashionably dressed genteel ladies, wearing red skirts, blue jackets, and blue hats with a white plume. They have a spirit of adventure for they are willing to dare a fairly brisk trot, sidesaddle.

Ten half-turns and the toy will send the riders trotting counterclockwise for nearly five minutes. This toy, so far, has not been located in any manufacturer's catalogue.

Maker unknown. c. 1880s. Tin clockwork toy, diameter 16"; horses and riders: 3½ x 4"

Right: This chase is led by a pretty cheerful-looking Brown Spotted Swine. In those days many individual homeowners raised a pig for food, and sometimes found it difficult to slaughter it when the time came since pigs, formerly symbolic of childhood happiness, are intelligent animals and can become pets.

The base is the familiar Fallows green with the diamond-shaped stamp and simple wheels.

Fallows. c. 1870. Tin, length 4½"

Center: The second figure is listed in the Stevens and Brown 1870 "Price List of Me-chanical Tin and Britannia Toys." As often happened, the tail on this horse differs from the line drawing in the catalogue, otherwise the details are the same. The horse resembles the horse of another manufacturer, which is possible because parts were exchanged among manufacturers. The horse is white with red harness; the jockey in black cap and boots wears a red coat and yellow trousers.

Stevens and Brown. 1870. Tin, length 6¼"

Left: The third figure is unidentified, but the horse is jumping with beautiful form.

Maker unknown. 1870s. Tin, length 9½"

Boy Hunting Raccoon

As the toy is pulled, the bell rings, warning the raccoon that someone is about. Movement of the wheels causes the boy to enter the hollow trunk and to back out as the usually peaceful but flesh-eating raccoon enters on the other side. This goes on as long as the child is content to pull the toy.

The boy wears a yellow shirt, red pants, and black shoes and hat. The raccoon and the tree are the same brownish color, perhaps painted with protective coloration in mind.

Gong Bell. 1880s. Cast iron, length 9″

Opposite: **Bird and Dog Squeak Toy**

A most unusual squeak toy: the bird, in flight, is mounted on a very sensitive spring rather than being attached to the platform. As the bellows is squeezed to produce the squeak, the bird—wings aflutter—quivers with fear as if to flee from danger. Also unusual is the fact that it is a small dog rather than a cat in pursuit of the gigantic robin.

The anonymous craftsman is believed to have come from Pennsylvania, influenced by German carvers who settled there.

Maker unknown. c. 1880. Papier-mâché (animals) and leather (bellows), length 6½″

138

FAIRY TALES AND FANTASY

Anything can happen in fairy tales: animals speak and are understood; tears can melt hard hearts and ice; toys locked in toy shops for the night step off the shelves, talk, walk, dance, sing, and love; bloodthirsty giants, dragons, and witches are beheaded by brave young people or vanish into space so that those they were tormenting can live happily ever after. Happiness, misery, violence, cupidity, love—all are ingredients, just as in real life, but in fairy tales, dreams and imagination run free.

There are many situations that are not easy for children to handle, but when a gingerbread boy can talk back to the world, in loud defiant tones, it helps children to release some of their anger. And when he is finally caught up with and eaten…well, isn't that what gingerbread boys are for?

Children faced with deep sorrow sometimes appear to skip over it; some, faced with what seem like insurmountable problems, deny them. Why not? Life is full of denials, beginning with a perhaps loving "Don't cry," which turns to a stern "Don't touch," and changes to a testy "Don't interrupt." The fact that these are justifiable "don'ts" from the adult point of view cannot really be of great validity to a young child. Perhaps the loveliest thing about fantasy and fairy tales is that they can be taken up and put down at will, repeated without danger—physical danger, that is.

Another wonderful quality of fairy tales is that they run pretty much according to stable rules: the good triumph and the bad meet their just rewards, and sometimes adult rules are bent. Children not only find

Daisy Bell Toy

The toy, described in the Gong Bell catalogue as "Girl with Doll on Sled with Chimes," is superbly cast, every inch beautifully detailed. Daisy wears a yellow coat; she is covered with a green quilt and keeps her hands warm in a tiny muff. Her doll is dressed in pink. As the toy is pulled a loud but pleasant chime is heard.

Gong Bell. Late 1890s. Cast iron, length 8¼"

Opposite: **Little Bo-Peep**

The catalogue description is "a pretty toy for young children, illustrating the nursery rhyme of Bo-Peep, the verses of which, with illustrations, accompany the toy, which is neatly packed in a neat wooden box." The sheep fit into grooves according to Crandall's 1867 building block patent. The toy was sold at $2.00 per dozen by the wholesaler and the suggested retail price was 25¢.

Charles M. Crandall. 1867. Wood, height: Bo-Peep, 6"; sheep, 2"

pleasure in fantasy play; they can make a world, temporary they know, in which justice is meted out and unfairness dealt with according to their lights. Thus they derive from fairy tales and fantasy play a sense of power and an inkling of their future roles when they will have left childhood behind them, will be able to cope with those bigger and stronger than they are, no longer dependent on adults or on fairy tales and fantasy solutions.

This is also true of the world of toys; children know that toys are not reality, that toys are in a sense instruments of fantasy and that they are playing. But what blissful removal from harsh reality—from situational problems with peers or parents—for the children who can manage dolls and homemaking toys as *they* please; or move solid construction toys and horses in vans, build skyscrapers and tumble them down...all representations of things that one day they may manage for real. And today, if sister chooses to play baseball and if brother plays with the dolls, many adults now accept that alternative role playing is not only natural but desirable.

The Old Woman That Lived in a Shoe

An Ives catalogue describes the "Mechanical Old Woman That Lived in a Shoe" as "a neatly painted, dressed old woman driver and a shoe full of children with patented trotting horse." The horse is known as the Cuzner Trotter (see page 156). When the clockwork is wound and released, a wire linking the motor with the horse's legs propels them in a trotting gait.

Ives. Late 1800s. Clockwork toy, length 15"

Opposite: **Ding Dong Bell**

This toy, representing the nursery rhyme, was cast in two pieces, joined in the center. Johnny Green who dropped the kitten down the well and Tommy Stout who bravely pulled her out are stationary, as is the cat, none the worse for the drenching. The bell is mounted in the well and rings as the toy is pulled along the floor. Note that the toy is called "Ding Dong Bell/ Pussy's NOT in the well," providing a happy twist to the nursery rhyme.

Gong Bell. c. 1900. Cast iron, length 9"

Opposite

Left: **Punch Cloth Toy**

The cloth Punch has usually been attributed to the same printworks that made the Thomas Nast Santa Claus (see page 151). However, in *Antiques of American Childhood*, Katharine McClinton states, "In September 1901 Punch and Judy dolls were used to promote the sale of blueing for the Textile Blueing Company whose New York address was next door to the Art Fabric Mills. So it is safe to say that Art Fabric Mills also made the Punch and Judy." This cannot be confirmed, but it is entirely possible. These printed figures usually had the company logo on the sheet; of course, this was separated from the figure when it was cut out.

A number of textile mills printed handkerchiefs, scarfs, squares to be used as doilies, and rag doll or animal figures to be cut out, stitched, and stuffed. Some were available only as premiums through the mail and made inexpensive, satisfying toys.

E. S. Peek (1880s) or Art Fabric Mills (1901). Cloth, height 15½"

Right: **Punch and Judy Mechanical Bank**

Judy holds a tray ready for a coin. When the lever is pressed, Punch rushes forward, club in hand, ready to bang poor Judy over the head. But thrift intervenes; Judy turns and deposits the coin safely. Several other manufacturers produced similar toys.

C. G. Shepard. Patented 1884. Cast iron, 7½ x 6¼"

Above: **Punch and Judy Animated Cap Pistol**

Judy is cast as a stationary figure at the end of the barrel; Punch is cast as part of the trigger; the cap receptacle is on Judy's back. When the trigger is released, Punch lunges forward, hits Judy on the back with his long nose, and the cap explodes.

Ives. 1882. Cast iron, length 5¾"

Below: **Humpty Dumpty Cap Exploders**

In the single exploder, one clown's head is part of the handle and is stationary; his open mouth provides the receptacle for the cap. When the handle is shaken the two heads come together: the long-nosed clown on the movable arm hits the other in the mouth, thereby exploding the cap.

The cap exploder with four faces, generally known as the Double Humpty Dumpty Animated Cap Exploder, has the same mechanism.

Ives. 1886. Cast iron with bronze japanned finish; single exploder: height 5"; double exploder: height 6"

145

The English in colonial New York took over the Dutch Saint Nicholas, patron saint of children, modified his name to Santa Claus, and moved his feast day from December 6 to coincide with Christmas. Some years later the rumor spread that Santa Claus could magically descend the chimney, pack and all, in a soot-proof suit. This did not seem to tax the credibility of most parents with their children, at least until they were ready to go off to school and be disillusioned by the wiser ones who had found a Santa suit in Daddy's closet, or presents not hidden carefully enough from their purposeful search.

Santa in Sleigh

The wooden toy manufacturers felt compelled to produce a Santa in a sleigh in order to compete with the tin and cast-iron models which sold so well, particularly at holiday time. The lithographed design is the same on both sides—drums, dolls, colorful balls, which were and still are the kinds of toys children get for Christmas.

Attributed to Bliss. Late 1800s. Lithographed paper on wood, length 12"

Santa Claus at Chimney

The action of this mechanical bank is most attractive. A coin is placed in Santa's raised hand; as the lever is pulled his hand is lowered and the coin slides down the chimney. The pack on Santa's back is filled with horns, whistles, and other toys. These are embossed into the casting of his pack.

J. and E. Stevens. Patented October 15, 1889. Cast iron, 6 x 4"

Overleaf: **Santa in Sleigh with Goats**

One of the larger toys of the period, it is unusual in that Santa has a composition face, a wooden body, and is dressed in crepe paper! It is among the most sought after by knowledgeable collectors. Only a few have been found; this one is complete and in its original condition.

When the toy is wound and the wheels are set in motion the goats move up and down, giving the impression that they are pulling the sleigh. The motion is occasioned by a special attachment from the rear legs of the goats to the wheel, which also causes the bells to jingle, making a pleasant sound.

Attributed to Althof, Bergmann. Late 1800s. Tin clockwork toy, 9 x 18"

147

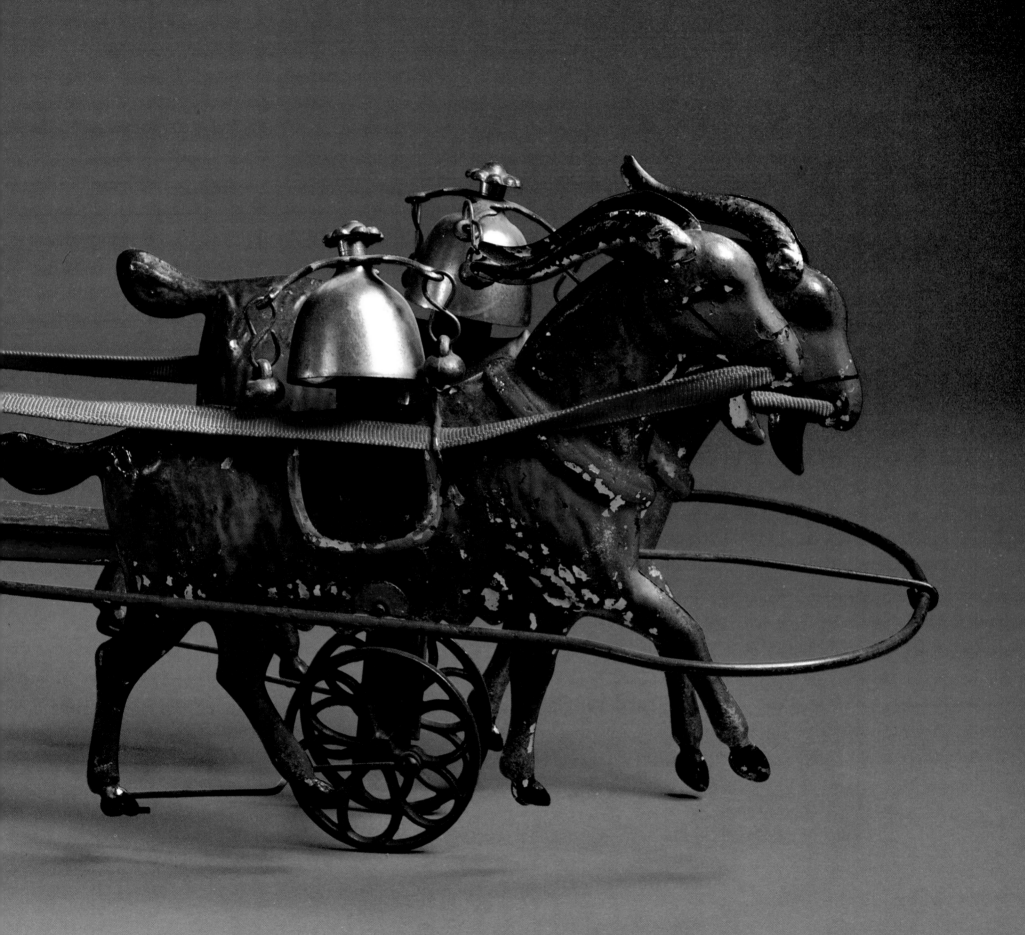

Opposite

Center: **Santa in Sleigh**

This beautifully cast Santa in Sleigh is an unusual design. Santa's half-body is attached to the sleigh, resting on a snow-covered blanket which appears to cover his legs *(see detail, left)*. The packages he is delivering are an integral part of the casting. The reindeer are considered the best designed and most interesting of any made in cast iron.

Kyser and Rex. c. 1800s. Cast iron, length 13"

Rear: **Santa Claus**

This fat, jolly Santa was copied from the Thomas Nast drawing, widely used by toy manufacturers and retailers in their Christmas advertisements in the late 1880s. According to Katharine McClinton in *Antiques of American Childhood*, this Santa was printed by E. S. Peek and sold by the New York Stationery and Envelope Company in 1886.

E. S. Peek. 1890s. Cloth, height 16½"

Right: **Walking Santa Claus**

This Santa is one of a series of cast-iron walking figures, all with the same body casting; only the faces are different. Among the others are "Ben Butler, Turk, Uncle Tom and Jackass." They were listed in the Oscar Strassburger (jobbers) catalogue for 1880 and ranged in price from $3.00 each for Butler to $3.75 for the Santa Claus. The figures were attractive and beautifully engraved; they were also expensive, which probably accounts for the fact that few are to be found today in collections or museums.

Ives. 1880s. Cast-iron clockwork toy, height 10"

STRICTLY FOR PLEASURE

Nineteenth-century America witnessed the birth and rapid growth of a new industry, the serious business of producing toys for children—strictly for pleasure. Early in the century, aside from some outdoor toys, very few children had any props specifically designed or manufactured to enhance their play. Boys usually had a bag of marbles ("miggies"), girls a small container of jackstones; both often had hoops. Most children had easy access to a rope for jumping or tug-of-war, a treasured potsy (hopscotch token), a wooden top, a willow whistle. Available, but harder to come by were a kite for spring winds, a sled in winter, a doll or knife, and in the yard a swing or seesaw.

As the century advanced, these outdoor activities began to appear as themes for the new toys, symbols of pleasure and the developing leisure hours. Fishing occupied much of a country boy's time in the summers. Usually it afforded approved idle hours in the sun and sometimes the catch even provided supper. Pull toys were made of boys fishing, of whales complete with Jonah, and of alligators. Leapfrog—"an excellent exercise if not indulged in too long as it is of a strenuous nature"—was introduced in a mechanical bank, as was jumping rope.

During the nineteenth century, well-to-do Victorian families took great pride in their fine horses and pleasure vehicles—phaetons, brakes, traps, and, for winter outings, sleighs. The new toy makers reproduced all of these for the pride and pleasure of the children.

Adults designed, manufactured, and marketed these toys for their own pleasure and profit, and adults now take pleasure in collecting the choice examples that have survived.

Detail of Man, Woman, and Boy in Horse-drawn Sleigh (see page 189).

153

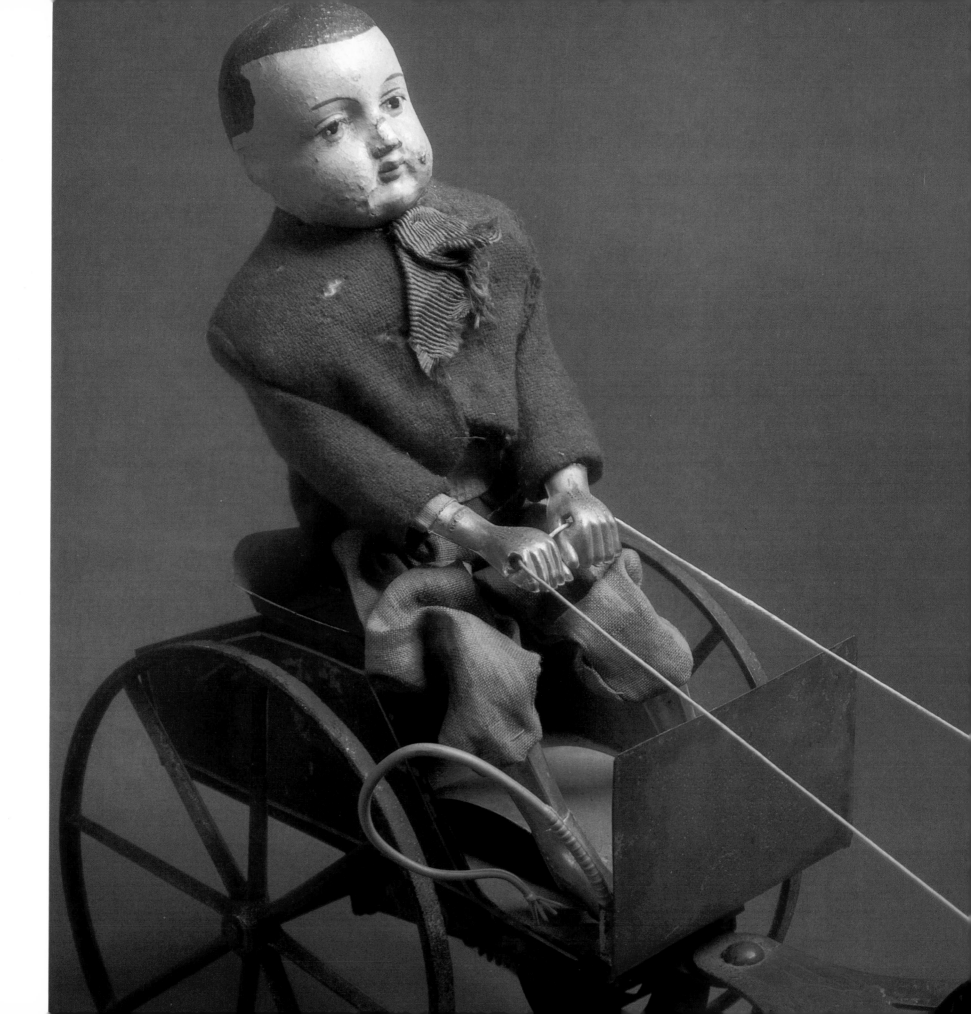

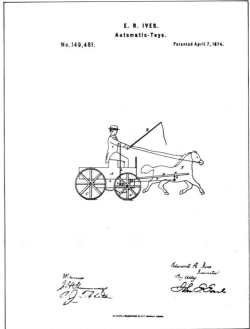

Top: **Mechanical Horse and Buggy with Whipping Driver**

When the toy is in motion the horse gallops; the driver's arm goes for all it is worth, whipping the horse to go faster. The manufacturer, who priced the toy at $3 per dozen (wholesale), describes it as "a pretty toy, strong and attractive." It *is* a most attractive toy. Being made on a larger scale than other clockwork horse and driver toys makes it a desirable collector's item.

Ives. 1874. Tin clockwork toy, length 17"

Bottom and opposite page *(detail):* **Cart Drawn by Two Horses**

In the 1870 George Brown Sketchbook this is #46 and is the largest clockwork toy they made. They used the figure from the clockwork tricycle shown on page 182 without alteration for this toy. The metal feet of the boy are molded tin and retain the loop on the soles of the shoes by which he was attached to the pedals of his tricycle. The horses' legs are attached to the wheel so that as the toy moves, the horses gallop.

George W. Brown. 1870. Tin clockwork toy, 10½ x 8"

Couple with Baby in Horse-drawn Buggy

The Durham (Connecticut) Historical Society has the same toy, but incomplete; an early Merriam catalogue shows this buggy and passengers pulled by *three* horses hitched in tandem. The young woman holding her baby adds much charm to a handsomely manufactured piece. She is dressed in white and wears a blue hat; the baby, without a hat, is dressed similarly. The father wears a red coat, with black trousers and hat.

The body of the buggy closely resembles the adult version, which is shaped like a grocer's coal box, so that people referred to it as "the coal-box buggy." Like its namesake, the toy buggy has a red interior, but the buggy is brown rather than black and its seat is yellow as opposed to the dark green of the family buggy.

Merriam. c. 1860. Tin, 4 x 8"

Cuzner Trotter

The trotter was patented in March, 1871, by J. Cuzner and named after him, a rare event. The patent was assigned to Ives for manufacture. The same carriage was also made with two team trotters. This tin clockwork toy was still carried in the Ives, Blakeslee and Williams catalogue c. 1893 and described as follows: "Dressed driver whips the horse and the horse trots in a very natural manner." The carriage is red. The driver is dressed in striped trousers, gray coat, and black hat.

Ives. 1871. Tin clockwork toy, length 12"

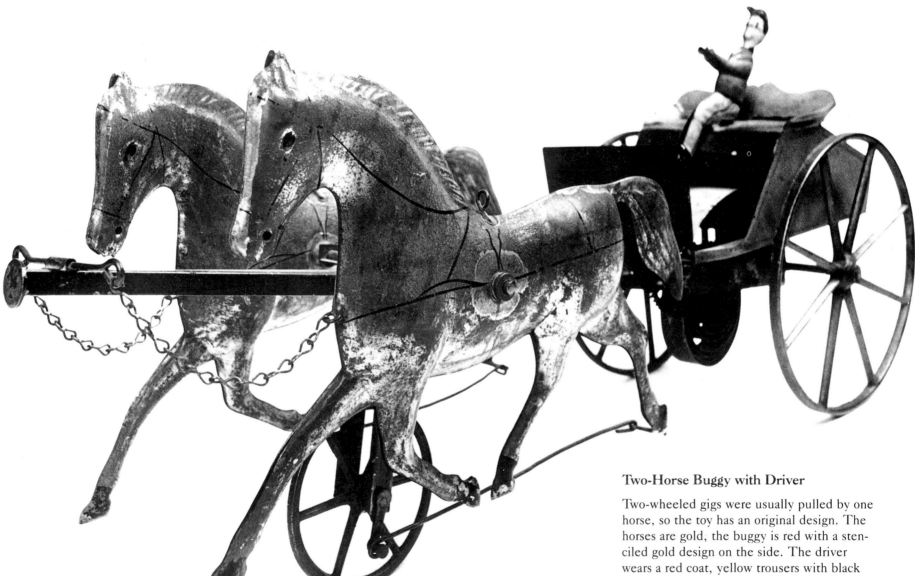

Two-Horse Buggy with Driver

Two-wheeled gigs were usually pulled by one horse, so the toy has an original design. The horses are gold, the buggy is red with a stenciled gold design on the side. The driver wears a red coat, yellow trousers with black stripe, and a black hat.

The whole toy is nearly identical to #49 in the George Brown Sketchbook, except that has only one horse. Because the shaft to which the horses are attached is slightly different from the other Brown toys, this is thought to be an earlier model, later redesigned to conform to the rest of the line for economy in production.

George W. Brown. 1870s. Tin, length 16"

Opposite: **Hansom Cab**

The hansom cab was a popular covered, fast-moving vehicle for one or two people. This imposing American Victorian house might have had such a cab in the carriage house, but they were originally designed as cabs for hire.

The brown horse has a white blanket and gold bridle. The cab is yellow with yellow wheels and black top. The coachman is also in yellow, with a black top hat.

Pratt and Letchworth. Late 1800s. Cast iron, length 12"

Tin Landaus

The coachman in the rear is nattily dressed in blue-gray trousers, black boots and jacket with red buttons. The other driver wears a red coat, yellow trousers. Both coaches are brown with gold stenciling. The door on the larger one opens.

Hull and Stafford. c. 1880s. Tin, length: rear toy, 19"; front toy, 10½"

Above

Front: **Rockaway**

The low-slung rockaway was a family carriage whose top covered the driver. It is red with a black top and a green interior. There are traces of gold paint on the horses' heads, and of gold stenciling on the side of the carriage.

Merriam. 1860s. Tin, length 12"

Rear: **Gig**

The gig was a sporting vehicle, considered too high for safe driving. It was often used to exercise a trotting horse. This gig has a red seat; the driver wears a black coat and tan trousers. He is urging on a white horse.

Hull and Stafford. Late 1860s–70s. Tin, length 12"

Opposite: **Mechanical Horses and Buggy with Dressed Driver**

Ives's tin buggies with their distinctive and beautifully designed patented galloping horses were made in two sizes: 12″ and 17″ long. Best sellers, they were also made with one or two horses, with or without whips and whipping drivers, differently dressed drivers, two-wheeled carts, and four-wheeled carriages; Ives got full mileage from this patent!

This example is a red buggy with yellow seat and one white horse. The driver is in typical checked trousers, red coat, and black hat with red band. The buggy was photographed in front of an 1829 New England tavern.

Ives. 1870s. Tin clockwork toy, length 12″

English Trap

The trap (from "trappings," connoting elegance) was more often found in the English or Irish countryside than in America. Very few toy companies manufactured it. This elegant-looking carriage was photographed in New Hampshire. The driver is dressed in a red coat, black trousers, and black derby; the coachman is in yellow with a black top hat and boots. The lady wears a blue skirt and hat and a red coat; the child is dressed in an orange suit with green hat. The horse and trap are plated in bronze.

Kenton. 1890s. Cast iron, length 15″

Barouche

A beautiful design, it exemplifies the type of good workmanship and meticulous attention to detail that went into the making of such toys. The horses are pale yellow with brown saddle blankets. The coach is black with gold upholstery, the wheels are rust color, striped in gold, and the coach lamp is black and red.

Pratt and Letchworth. 1890s. Cast iron, length 17"

Lady with Dog in Phaeton

This graceful phaeton is slightly larger than usual. The horse and carriage are black; the wheels are red; the coachman is attired in correct formal black uniform. The lady wears a yellow coat and brown skirt.

Kenton. Late 1800s. Cast iron, length 18"

Phaeton

Here is a "ladies' phaeton," a sports model to be driven by the owner. It was also available without fenders and in a lighter-weight material. The unusual coloring—white carriage, red wheels, and black horse—is striking.

Hubley. Late 1800s. Cast iron, length 17"

Four-Passenger Surrey with Two Horses

A Welker and Crosby catalogue describes this toy, originally patented in 1883: "Its imitation of the original surrey is so perfect, the movements of the horses so accurate, and its finish so beautiful that it cannot fail to please every child in the land." All the Welker and Crosby toys show meticulous design and casting with careful attention to detail.

The Welker and Crosby swivel wheel is slightly different from those of other manufacturers of cast-iron toys; it also varies from the improved wheel in the 1885 patent, or second edition. The fact that the horses and other features are almost identical to those of Pratt and Letchworth leads one to speculate that Pratt and Letchworth used the Crosby patents and designs under some licensing or royalty agreement. Mr. Crosby of the Welker and Crosby Company was employed by Pratt and Letchworth in 1889.

Welker and Crosby. Patented 1883. Malleable iron, length 15"

Brougham

This elegant closed carriage with the driver's seat outside was named after Lord Henry Peter Brougham, the young Scottish Liberal leader of the House of Commons in the 1830s and 1840s.

To suit a variety of tastes, this brougham was also made in a larger size, with or without the driver (presumably one had one's own) in a choice of colors—green, blue, or red. A beautiful toy of a bygone era, photographed in front of Independence Hall in Philadelphia.

Merriam. Early 1870s. Tin, length 11"

165

Overleaf: **Tally-ho and Brakes**

This photograph could have been taken in the 1880s or 1890s when groups of friends went for a "jolly country outing" or to the races in their tally-hos. Undoubtedly only the children of the well-to-do could reflect such a custom in their toys.

Right and left: **Two- and Three-Seated Brake**

The Two-Seated Brake is known to exist in only a few collections. This one has three passengers and a driver.

The high, open Three-Seated Brake was also produced in a 20½"-long as well as in a 28"-long, four-horse model carrying seven passengers and a driver.

Hubley. c. 1900. Cast iron, Two-Seated Brake: length 17"; Three-Seated Brake: length 18"

Center: **Tally-ho Coach #555**

This Carpenter Tally-ho, one of the most beautiful cast-iron toys ever manufactured, has its original paint, passengers, and driver. The specially designed wheel on the Carpenter horses gives them the best galloping action among movable horses. Patented in 1880, the Tally-ho was still featured in an 1892 catalogue of XL (Carpenter) toys. In Ehrich's 1891–92 holiday jobbers' catalogue, the Tally-ho listed for $4.98 each, wholesale.

Carpenter. 1880. Cast iron, length 26"

Opposite

Right: **Pony Cart**

The lady, wearing a blue skirt and bonnet and red jacket, is driving a model of an 1880s pony cart (or road cart), a light but well-balanced vehicle for pleasure driving.

Shimer. 1890s. Cast iron, length 10"

Left: **Man in Horse-drawn Dog Cart**

Dog carts were originally used for carrying hunting dogs to meets. They were fashionable, lightweight, and had good storage space under the seats.

Pratt and Letchworth. 1890s. Cast iron, length 13¾"

Above: **Ives Hansom Cab**

A singularly large and sturdy hansom cab, it featured a shaft that opened on one side so that the horse could be taken out of harness and played with separately or put into the stall in its stable. The carriage is black with ornate gold trim, light tan horse, red wheels, and—rubber tires! Ives also made the same hansom cab without the rubber tires. They gave this toy a luxurious touch.

Ives. Late 1800s. Cast iron, length 15"

Right: **Spider Phaeton**

Spider phaetons were made by several cast-iron toy manufacturers with two styles available, one with the carriage alone and the model shown with a rumble seat for the coachman. But the casting is fragile, particularly where the coachman's seat is attached, so few have survived intact.

Hubley. Late 1800s. Cast iron, length 15"

Tops

All the tops vary slightly in design, shape, striping, or color. A small piece has been chopped from the back of each top so as to have it lie flat on the display board, which may have been designed by a salesman for convenience in carrying his samples or used as a display in a factory or agent's salesroom. Labels with prices are mounted beside each top.

Ives. c. 1885. Wood, tops: length from 2¼" to 4"; the wood board on which they are mounted is 6½ x 12¾"

Girl Spinning Top

Here is a charming watercolor of a little girl sitting at her tea table, of all things, spinning a top! Tops were generally considered toys for boys, but the little girl pictured, like the girls of ancient Greece and Rome, was obviously fascinated by the spinning top.

Painter unknown. c. 1890. Watercolor, 4¼ x 6½"

Opposite: **Tops**

The top has been known to every recorded civilization. In the Midwest, top-spinning contests are still held in the spring. They have a fascination for adults and children alike. Children have top games, spinning them in the palms of their hands, throwing the top to a target; older children and adults wager as to who can throw the longest spin.

These early American tops are hand-painted, unusually well balanced, and as representative of beautiful toys as they are of the wood-working skills of the person who made them.

Makers unknown. c. 1880. Wood, length: top on the left, 7½"; the other two, each 5½"

Opposite: **Football Bank**

The words "A Calamity" are cast in the base of the bank; since there are other banks known as the "Football Bank," this one, patented by James H. Bowen, is usually referred to as the "Calamity Bank."

The bank is beautifully cast on a green platform and red base. The players are in yellow uniforms, but the tackles have red jerseys and socks while the fullback wears blue. He seems to be the calamity and the red-shirts seem to be getting the applause of the crowd. For the bank to work, the right and left tackles must be moved into position and the coin placed in front of the fullback. When the lever is pressed the players come together in a huddle; the fullback fumbles and the coin drops into the bank.

J. and E. Stevens. Patented 1891. Cast iron, 6½ x 7½"

Fowler Bank

This is perhaps one of the rarest banks ever produced. The late John Meyer, dean of mechanical bank collectors, describes the action of the Fowler: "figure of a hunter swings his gun around and shoots at bird which flies away when the spring is released." The coin, placed in a slot to the right of the hunter's foot, disappears inside when the hunter fires his gun. For realism the hammer of the rifle can be pulled back to insert a paper cap which really explodes with a satisfying bang when the gun is fired.

J. and E. Stevens. Patented 1892. Cast iron, length 9"

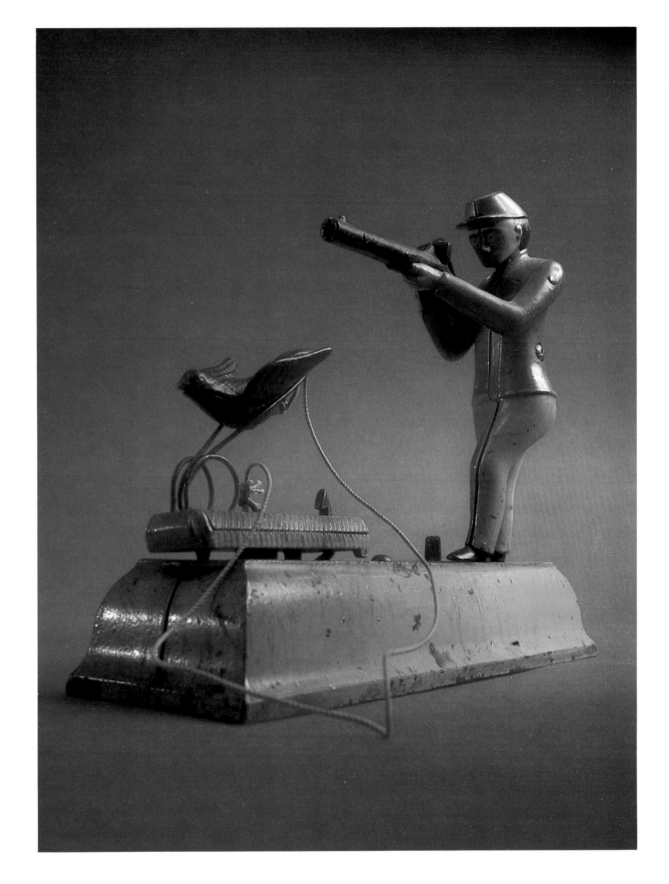

Opposite: **Leap-Frog Bank**

The leaper is dressed in blue pants, yellow shirt, red belt, and red socks; the bending boy has a blue shirt, red pants and cap. As one boy leaps over the other he strikes a lever which drops the coin into the bank.

In an 1852 book called *Games and Sports,* boys were told "there is no better exercise for the limbs than leap frog but too violent to be continued for a long time."

C. G. Shepard. Patented September 15, 1891. Cast iron, length 7½"

Girl-Skipping-Rope Mechanical Bank

The flaxen-haired girl wears a white dress, green apron, and red bow. The intricately cast bank is equally colorful in red, yellow, green, and blue. The girl skips rope and the coin is deposited in the slot on the right; the coin plays no part in the action as in most mechanical banks. Originally produced at $1.50 wholesale, it was probably too expensive to be sold in large quantities. It was listed in the Montgomery Ward mail-order catalogue of 1894.

J. and E. Stevens. Patented April 15, 1890. Cast iron, height 8"

Opposite: **Champion Velocipede**

Both Jesse and Charles M. Crandall had patented velocipedes for children to ride in 1868, possibly after they had seen one patented by Lallement in Paris in 1866. These were immensely popular. The following year there was a rash of toy velocipede patents: one taken out by E. Eaton of Hartford on May 4, 1869; four by A. M. Allen between June, 1869–June, 1870; one by N. S. Warner in September, 1869, which was produced by Ives; and several others.

This velocipede was an instant success, appearing not only in jobbers' catalogues but also in retail catalogues and ads. It was offered for sale by Althof, Bergmann, and was illustrated in the Stevens and Brown catalogue of 1872 (see page 183). A rod attached to a rear wheel causes the driver to steer alternately right and left, repeating the action until the motor winds down. The blonde young lady was photographed in front of a lovely Victorian house in Cape May, New Jersey.

Stevens and Brown. Patented 1870. Clockwork toy, 5½ x 10"

Girl on Velocipede and **Monkey on Velocipede**

Both toys, among the first mechanical toys in the Ives line, work on the same principle as the Uncle Sam on Velocipede (see page 71). "When the clockwork is wound the monkey works the levers to the manner born—in a straight line or in a large circle to suit his fancy."

Both toys: Ives. c. 1875. Tin clockwork toys, height 9"

Opposite

Center: **Kaleidoscope**

The front end of the cylinder resembles a ship's pilot wheel. The inside is lined with bits of mirror and small objects. When the cylinder is turned, the toy produces an infinite variety of designs.

C. C. Bush. Patent reissued 1873. Length 11"

Left, rear: **Candle**

The candle in the simple black tin box was designed to provide light for a kaleidoscope.

A. D. Handy. 1880s. Height 9½"

Left, front: **Stereoscope and Views**

The smallest stereoscope ever produced, it boasts of having "one hundred views of happy scenes of children and a complete and natural history of wild and domestic animals, making an entertaining and delightful hour for little folks." There are fifty cards, printed on both sides.

The Metropolitan Syndicate Press. c. 1890. Stereoscope: length 4¼"; cards: 1 x 4"

Right: **Symmetroscope**

Two mirrors set at angles to each other at the bottom of this toy create a kaleidoscopic effect as objects on the disk at the bottom are rotated.

The Wale-Irving Company. Patented March, 1899. Height 6½"

Below

Right: **Zoetrope**

The Zoetrope or Wheel of Life consists of a drum, with an evenly spaced series of slits, on a wood spindle and base. After the drum was set spinning, one looked through the slits: the man seemed to be riding a bicycle! These were animated pictures; startling for 1867. The Zoetrope was sold with twelve strips, each one different; many others were available.

Milton Bradley. Patented 1867. Height 7"

Left: **Praxinoscope**

The Praxinoscope or Whirligig of Life was originally designed in France. Its working resembled the Zoetrope, but the illusion of movement was created with mirrors. It too came with a set of twelve chromolithographed strips; others were available.

Mc Loughlin Brothers. 1870s. Height 6"

Left: Girl on Swing

The Girl on Swing is known as the Warner Toy. A colorfully dressed figure, she sits on the swing and is propelled forward and backward. The National Toy Company, representatives for the Ives Company and several other manufacturers, described it as "a very fine toy for showing in your window." The same toy was also made with a boy standing on the swing seat. Both sold for $25 per dozen wholesale, a fairly expensive toy during its time.

Ives. 1870s. Clockwork toy, height 14"

Center: Toy Seesaw

The Boy and Girl on Seesaw was patented by Albert H. Dean of Bridgeport, Connecticut, November 25, 1873, and assigned to the Ives Company. The catalogue description reads: "a very attractive toy with exceedingly natural movements. It runs for half an hour at one winding." This toy and the Girl on Swing are run on the same type of clockwork.

Ives. 1873. Clockwork toy, length 18"

Right: Boy on Tricycle

The American Toy Company, located in New York, was the distributor for Stevens and Brown. Its 1872 catalogue describes the Champion Velocipede in glowing terms: "No toy has ever been put upon the market which has been received with more general acceptance. Its evolutions being perfectly automatic, it is a source of amusement equally to the child and the adult." The front wheel turns so that it can be made to go straight or around in a circle. The same toy has been found with both boy and girl riders, black as well as white, in different costumes. It cost $24 per dozen wholesale.

Stevens and Brown. Patented 1870. Clockwork toy, length 11"

A. H. DEAN.
Automatic Toys.

No. 144,892.

Patented Nov. 25, 1873.

Baby Quieter Bell Toy

A humorous toy—when pulled, the man, comfortably stretched out on a chaise longue with baby on his leg, plays a game such as "This is the way the babies ride" or "Ride a cock-horse to Banbury Cross" in the hope that it will keep the baby quiet. Father is reading the "Evening News Baby Quieter." He also prudently holds in his right hand, out of sight, a rattle to amuse the baby when he tires of this game.

The toy is beautifully cast with intricate detail in the man's clothing as well as in the upholstery of the chaise.

Gong Bell. 1890s. Cast iron, length 7½"

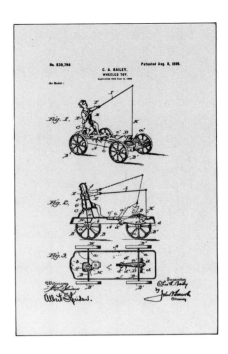

Boy Fishing Bell Toy

An exceptionally colorful toy: the boy is wearing a tan hat, mustard-yellow shirt, red trousers, and black boots. The base is an unusual aquamarine, the fish is silver, and the wheels are yellow.

The catalogue describes this "automatic" pull toy: "As the toy moves, the boy, feeling a bite, jerks the fish from the water." Trying to inject a bit of humor into the catalogue copy, the writer added, parenthetically, "no landing net required." The toy sold for 25¢.

N. N. Hill Brass. c. 1900. Cast iron, 5½ x 6½"

Double Oarsman

The Single Oarsman can be found in a number of collections, but this Double Oarsman is currently believed to be much rarer. It bears the same patent date as the Single Oarsman, February 9, 1869. Ives also featured a Mechanical Parlor Oarsman with wheels to run on the floor.

Ives. 1870s. Tin clockwork toy, length 19"

Boy Sailboat Bell Toy

This early tin toy is the only one known to this collector. As the cast-iron wheels are turned, the green boat moves into the wind, tin sail furled, rocking gently as the bell buoy rings.

Hull and Stafford(?). c. 1860s. Tin, 10½ x 9"

Opposite: **Mechanical Oarsman**

Listed by the National Toy Company in its catalogue for 1870: "the figure . . . will pull the boat on any sheet of water or in a wash tub, bathtub or basin for a distance of about 500 feet. It works naturally and is truly a scientific toy. $28 per dozen, wholesale."

This oarsman is resting in a small tidal marsh on the Housatonic River, not far from the factory in which the toy was produced.

Ives. Patented February, 1869. Clockwork toy, length: boat, 12"; oars, 7"

Below: Both toys are most unusual; wheeled vehicles of all kinds were usually portrayed, but sleighs are definitely out of the ordinary.

Boy in Sleigh Pulled by Goats

Althof, Bergmann. Late 1800s. Tin, length 10"

Man, Woman, and Boy in Horse-drawn Sleigh

Hull and Stafford. Late 1800s. Tin, length 16"

Overleaf: **Horses and Riders**

Here are six equestrians out for an early morning ride in the country. The toy on the extreme left is unusual in that the man and woman are riding side by side, on separate horses mounted on a single base. In the lead (extreme right) is a very rare clockwork toy. Although it was made by Stevens and Brown, the figures of the woman and horse are identical to those of the toys made by Hull and Stafford. Here again is incontrovertible proof that the early tin toy makers were neighborly shops and that they exchanged all kinds and sizes of parts according to their needs.

From left to right:

Hull and Stafford. 1870s. Tin, length 8¾"

Maker unknown. 1870s. Tin, length 6"

Hull and Stafford. 1870s. Tin, length 8¾"

Hull and Stafford. 1870s. Tin, length 8¾"

Stevens and Brown. 1870s. Tin clockwork toy, length 8"

Above: **Boy on Sleigh**

As the toy is pulled along the floor the horses move forward, then backward; the boy in the sleigh is stationary. The boy wears a brown hat and yellow shirt; his pants are painted bright orange to match the sleigh. Like the other eight Fallows "Moveable Combination Toys," it has a base which hides the mechanism. This toy wholesaled at $27 per gross, less than 19¢ apiece.

Fallows. Patented 1886. Tin, length 9½"

Below: **Double Ripper Sled Bell Toy**

As the sled speeds over the snow the bell rings to clear the way. This toy and the "Watermelon Bell Toy" were the most expensive in the line, wholesaling for 50¢; the rest of the toys were 10¢ and 25¢.

N. N. Hill Brass and Watrous. c. 1900. Cast iron, length 8¾"

Opposite: **Movable Horses and Riders**

The action of this toy is semimechanical: there are thin rods hooking up the two front horses to the front axle and the other rider to the rear axle. As the wheels turn the horses run at a gallop. It is unusual to find a tin toy of this period with such action; most were either clockwork or pull toys with stationary figures.

Hull and Stafford. 1870s. Tin, 8½ x 11"

Old Colored Fiddler

The fiddler is richly dressed: white shirt, velvet morning coat, black-and-white checked trousers. His fiddle is made of wood; he plays with a metal bow. A special attachment to the clockwork moves the fiddler's bow from right to left across the threadlike strings.

Probably made by the Automatic Toy Works with the design taken over by Ives. 1880s or earlier. Clockwork toy, height 9½"

Mechanical Cakewalk Dancers

Most of the Ives mechanical dancers have cast-iron hands and feet. The Cakewalkers have more neatly made and proportioned hands and feet, of wood; the heads are composition. The woman's dress is tan and blue with matching tan hat. The man's coat is blue, his knee pants and hat orange.

An Ives catalogue c. 1890 calls this toy a "Splendid Window Attraction," and describes it as "two dressed figures of colored society people, so arranged that when the toy is wound, the figures will dance in a lively and comical manner." Had Ives called them vaudeville dancers he would have been more accurate; the costumes are those of stage entertainers, suitable for an amusing toy. These "attractive, substantial novelties . . . comical, full of life and motion" wholesaled at $36 per dozen.

Automatic Toy Works. c. 1870s. Clockwork toy, 10 x 8 x 8"

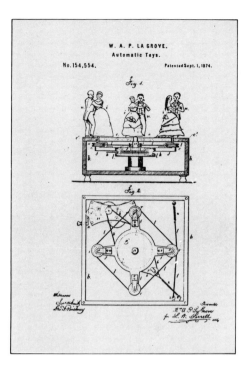

Opposite: **The Dancers**

These charming wooden dancers might well have been copied from an idea patented in 1874 by one William La Grové *(above)* which he described as automatic "Toy Dancers"—or did Mr. La Grove get his idea from this folk toy?

When the crank on the right is turned, the pulley system is activated and the platform revolves. The cord may be attached to the individual platforms so that one couple at a time can perform. The dancers are simply dressed—the men in shirts and trousers painted in reds, blues, and greens, the ladies in shirtwaists and skirts of the same colors.

Folk toy. Maker unknown; probably from Ohio. Late 1800s. Wood, box: 7 x 12½ x 12½"; figures: height 3½" and 4½"

Maypole Dancers Bell Toy

A unique design gives movement to the platform on which the May Day figures are dancing. As the toy is pulled or pushed, the four girders that support the dancing floor above the platform of the toy move while the bell rings. This quite possibly was a centennial toy: the dancers are patriotically dressed in red, white, and blue.

Althof, Bergmann. 1880s. Tin, 9¼ x 11"

THE CIRCUS

Small traveling circuses went from town to town throughout Europe and the United States from the 1830s on. Sometimes these consisted of a lone clown, sometimes a gypsy wagon and a family or group of performers, sometimes a tent, acrobats, and a sawdust ring for performing animals.

P. T. Barnum got his start in 1834 with an exhibition of a black slave billed as the 161-year-old nurse of George Washington. Everyone knew it was a fraud but came anyway, encouraging Barnum to deal in fakes, which he did, with notable exceptions: as impresario for Jenny Lind in 1850 and as promoter of General Tom Thumb. Vernon Parrington, the great American historian, writes in *Main Currents in American Thought*, vol. 3 (1930), that Barnum was "the very embodiment" of the Gilded Age, "growing rich on the profession of humbuggery, a vulgar greasy genius, pure brass without any gilding."

After the Civil War, James Bailey introduced the huge tent with three rings, the "three-ring circus" that we know today. He joined with Barnum to promote the most famous American circus—Barnum and Bailey's "Greatest Show on Earth." It provided a transcontinental entertainment for all the people and their children. Naturally such a popular activity attracted the attention of toy designers, always alert to any trend that could be reproduced in the toy world. The circus theme has been and continues to be a rich-flowing source of children's toys, from the early tin to the current plastic performers. From 1850 on, circus toys were made in some form by all big and not-so-big toy companies. Favorites among

Acrobat with Horses on Ferris Wheel

The Ferris wheel is gracefully mounted on a center core reminiscent of colonial candle-molds. The controlling mechanism keeps all the pretty little horses level as the Ferris wheel turns. The acrobat seems to be trying to decide on which horse he will leap.

Because the acrobat and the 4"-long horses with distinctive tails are the same as those on other Hull and Stafford toys, this is presumed to be a Hull and Stafford toy. The horses are white with black reins and red cinch belts.

Hull and Stafford. 1870s. Tin, height 13½",
diameter 8½"

199

collectors are the often photographed Hubley and Kenton cast-iron wagons and the jointed wooden Schoenhut circus, complete with tent.

We have endeavored to select and identify circus toys that are seen less often, some of which cannot be linked positively to a particular manufacturer. This is a difficult task among early tin toys, for which tinsmiths so often exchanged parts. For example, they perhaps stamped or molded their own horses but bought wheels and other forms from some other shop; and shops are what some of the creators of the rarest collectors' toys worked in. While it is true that some of these toys were "mass-produced," it is well to remember that mass production before the 1850s yielded an infinitesimal quantity in comparison with today's enormous output.

This circus group is ready to enter the ring and perform.

Right and left: Monkey on Horse and Monkey on Elephant

The twin monkeys are dressed in green with red caps. The two pull toys are mounted on Fallows green bases and have the same wheels of absolutely plain design used by Fallows.

The black horse with gold reins is stationary. The elephant's trunk is jointed and moves in true elephant fashion. The toy benefits from an ingenious Fallows patent (June 5, 1883)—a miter bar attached to one front wheel so that as the wheels turn the bar hits a spring attached to a clapper that strikes a bell hidden under the platform.

Fallows. 1800s. Tin, Monkey on Horse: length 6¼"; monkey, height 3"; Monkey on Elephant: 6½ x 7"; monkey, height 3¼"

Center: Performing Dog

The base and wheels on this unusual Performing Dog appear to be the same as those of the monkey riders, but the toy is attributed to Althof, Bergmann. The dog is white.

Attributed to Althof, Bergmann. 1880s. Tin, base: length 3"; dog: height 2½"

Rear: Acrobats in Hoop

Most hoop toys of this date are small (6–7" in diameter) and generally encircle a familiar animal. This one is unusual on two counts: it is one of the largest of its day (12" in diameter and 2¾" wide) and the figures within are boy and girl acrobats, with a happy animal director. The ornate cut-out band of the hoop is of antique design. As the hoop is rolled the acrobats remain upright, suspended in mid-air performance on their narrow platform.

While the boy wears a painted green suit and red cap, the girl's costume is red with yellow trim and has the lustrous finish of japanned ware, as does the monkey's blue-green suit and brown cap. In outline the monkey in this hoop seems to belong with the other two. However, it is not only of slightly different design, but is made of one piece of rolled (flat) tin while the others are both made of two pressed (molded) pieces, joined, which gives them the third lifelike dimension.

Attributed to Fallows. c. 1880. Tin, diameter 12"; acrobats: height 4½"; monkey: height 2¾"

Acrobat

This delightful toy, an amusing carving of a man doing circus acrobatics on his horse, is very fragile. It is held together by small tacks.

Folk art. Maker unknown; probably from Pennsylvania. c. 1880. Wood, 9 x 7½"

Opposite: Detail of Single Acrobat *(see following page).*

Mechanical Acrobats

Acrobats have always been a popular and featured act of every circus, so it seems logical that toy designers would create an appealing toy around this familiar theme. The challenge was how to give it animation. This became a simple design problem when they decided to use clockwork springs. They could be geared for forward and backward motion which would allow the acrobats, as one catalogue describes it, to do "all that any living acrobat can do."

The single acrobat on turning bar *(see detail, preceding page)* and the man and woman acrobats have wooden bodies, the men with composition heads and metal hands, the woman with china head and hands. The two male acrobats on a single bar have wooden bodies, composition heads, and thin, flat, loosely attached legs. As the motor turns clockwise, then counterclockwise, the acrobats perform a variety of stunts. The free motion of their legs and their whimsical expressions make this an amusing and entertaining toy.

Careful attention was paid to the dress of the male gymnasts; they wear the type of clothing acrobats of the period wore when performing. They also have handlebar mustaches that were fashionable in the Victorian period. The lady acrobat wears a green costume with lace collar and red high shoes, her companion a green shirt with lace collar and knee-length red trousers. The two men acrobats wear red and yellow trunks and red and yellow caps.

Right: **Single Acrobat**

Ives. Patented April 13, 1875. Clockwork toy, 8 x 7"

Center: **Man and Woman Acrobats**

Automatic Toy Works. 1870s. Clockwork toy, 9 x 10"

Left: **Two Men on Bar**

Ives. 1880s. Clockwork toy, 7 x 6"

Crandall's Lively Horseman

An ad in *Youth's Companion* of October 30, 1879, run by the Orange Judd Co., New York City jobbers, described this pull toy as "the most comical and pleasing mechanical toy ever seen. There is no clockwork to get out of order. It is strongly made, prettily painted, not easily broken and can be taken apart and packed in the box on which they perform. It represents Barnum's circus rider to perfection."

The mounted clown is attached to the horse's reins—two lively springs. The hind legs of the horse are attached to the wheels by a concealed wooden rod so that the horse bucks as the box is pulled, while the clown performs an infinite variety of acrobatic stunts.

Charles M. Crandall. Patented 1879. Wood, container: 10¼ x 4"; clown: height 12¾"

Below

Left: **Comic Parlor Hippodrome**

On July 21, 1874, Jesse Armour Crandall, cousin of Charles M., patented a "jointed doll." The joint was a simple metal clip designed to slide anywhere onto wood that was ¼" thick. The body parts are all ¼" thick; the torsos are lithographed but delightfully interchangeable; the combinations are unlimited. One set, packed in a wooden box with sliding top *(see following page)*, contained sufficient clips and parts to make one horse and five acrobatic figures.

Jesse Crandall. 1874. Lithographed wood, assembled horse: height 6"; assembled acrobat: height 9"

Right: **Crandall's Acrobats**

This toy was advertised in December, 1874, in the New York *Daily Graphic:* "Full of fun and frolic and most brilliant in costume. These are among the most fascinating and ingenious toys ever invented. The number of figures that can be made with the pieces in a single box is

limited only by the ingenuity of the operator." A November ad in the *American Agriculturist* claimed that about 1500 boxes of Acrobats were being shipped daily, so great was the demand!

Each piece had five continuous grooves so that it could be joined almost anywhere without connectors. Too many connectors got lost from Crandall's Hippodrome, thus rendering the toy useless.

Charles M. Crandall. 1874. Lithographed wood, assembled acrobat: height 8"

Opposite: **Barnum's Menagerie**

One of the nicest made by any of the manufacturers, this lion wagon cage has the standard punched-tin design that appears on so many other tin toys. The effect is very pleasing; the red, white, and blue colors add to its attractiveness and lend a patriotic touch to an entertainment very popular at the time.

Merriam. 1880s. Tin, 8¾ x 13½"

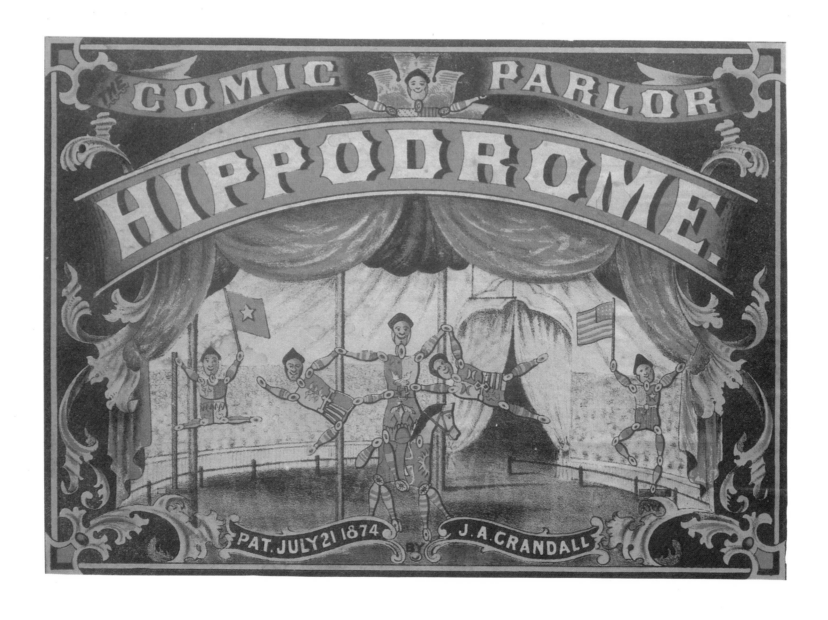

Top: **Clown on Powder Keg**

The same clown casting is used on both cap pistols. Although the Clown on Powder Keg is not a spring-operated cap gun, it is usually part of animated cap pistol collections. The barrel simply serves to hold the powder keg, into which one puts a small firecracker. When it explodes, it blasts the clown off the keg and he falls forward, dead, on the barrel of the pistol.

Ives. 1880s. Cast iron, length 3¾"

Bottom: **Mule and Clown**

As the pistol is cocked, a cap is placed on the seat of the pants of the clown, who is an integral part of the casting. The trigger extends above and below the barrel of the pistol; when the lower trigger is pulled, the upper one propels the mule's hind legs so that it kicks the seat of the clown's pants, which explodes the cap. Both toys express pratfall humor.

Ives. 1880s. Cast iron, length 5"

208

Opposite: **Elephant and Three Clowns Mechanical Bank**

Interestingly, a patent for this bank was issued in England about ten days earlier than in the United States. In 1883, the manufacturer described the bank: "Place the coin between the rings held by the acrobat. Move the ball on the feet of the other acrobat, and the Elephant will strike the coin with his trunk, which will cause it to fall into the receptacle below. At the same time the Clown on the Elephant will face about."

J. and E. Stevens. Patented 1882. Cast iron, 5 x 5½"

Above: **Clown Bell Ringers**

One right-handed and one left-handed clown sit back to back on a mule. As the toy is drawn across the floor, the mule bucks so that first one clown and then the other dips his striker into the bell. The rare wheels have two engaging acrobats turning cartwheels for spokes.

Gong Bell. c. 1900. Cast iron, length 9½"

Overleaf: **Circus parade** of tin toys manufactured in the 1860s and 1870s. With the exception of the circus wagon, which is 14" long, the toys measure 8" to 10".

The leopard in the wagon cage on the far right (center row) was made by George Brown. The other two wagon cages are products of Merriam. The Horse and Rider (last row, left), the Camel to its right, the Monkey on Elephant (last row, right), the Elephant (extreme left), and the Chariot (front row, second from left) were all made by Fallows. The small figures on base and wheels (front row, left, and second from right) and the balancing figure (front row, left) are also George Brown toys. The figure on the rounded base (front row, right) is attributed to Althof, Bergmann.

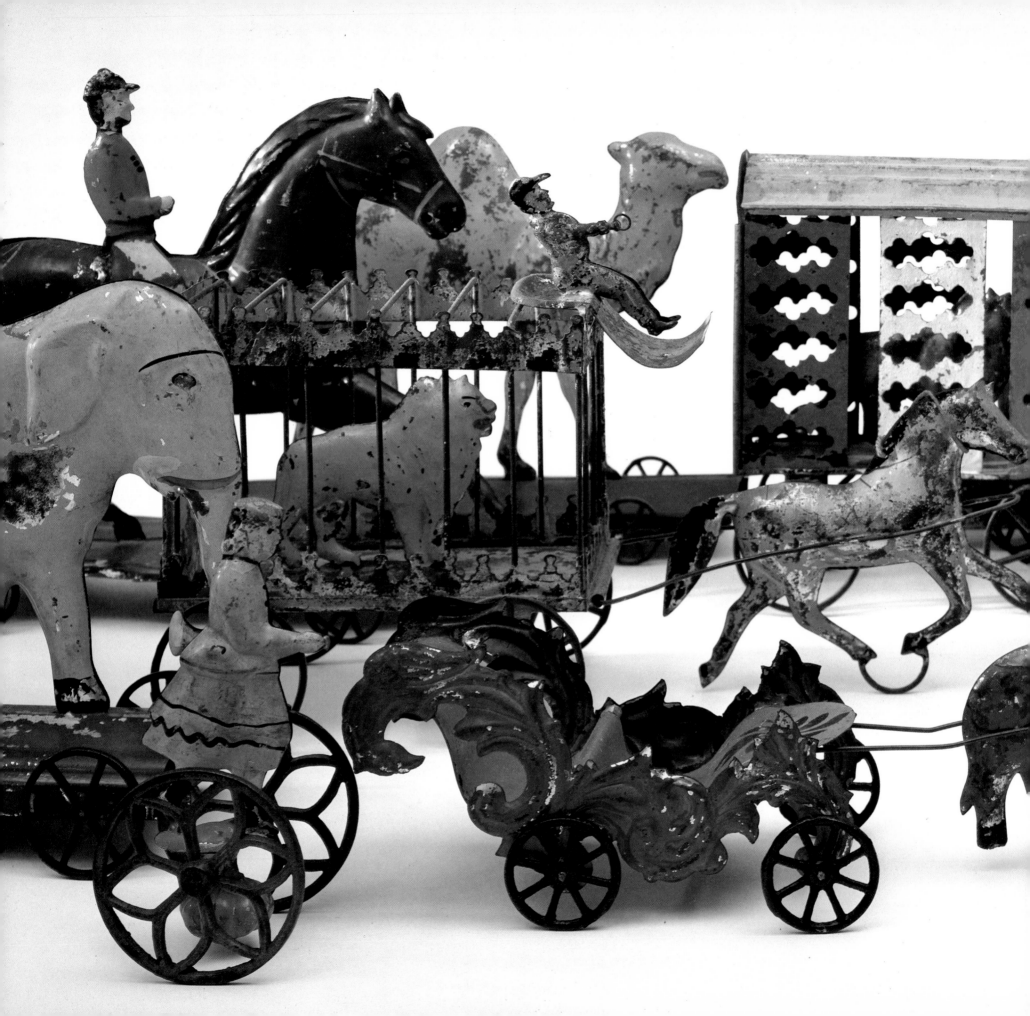

New Exhibition Wagon

Reed hit upon a most seductive advertising slogan for the circus toys: "Every boy his own showman." This toy represents the lead wagon in the parade that announced to the town residents that the circus was set up and ready to perform. The lithographed box has a sliding top which allows for all the parts to be disassembled and packed inside. When set up, the box top becomes an integral part of the toy on which flags, flyers, ads, and other attachments can be fitted.

W. S. Reed. Patented May 14, 1878. Lithographed paper on wood, box: 4 x 13"

Opposite: **Trained Menagerie**

Left: A most unusual pull toy of circus animal performers and their trainers. In addition to the green platform on wheels, a small wheel is attached to the center of each axle. The trainer and lion and the trainer and horse are each secured to the base and pole. The center pole is made of rolled tin and fits over a 2" metal rod attached to the wheeled base of the toy. As the toy is pulled the wheels attached to the center of the axle revolve, causing the trainers and their animals to make a 360° turn.

The two trainers wear red suits and black caps.

Center: The Dog on Ladder is fixed in place. The base to which it is attached has the same rolled-tin construction as the pull toy. The ladder is white, the dog (also used for the Performing Dog on page 201), brown.

Right: The Trainer and Leopard is made like all the other parts. The trainer wears a blue suit and a black cap; the leopard is brown.

Perhaps the pull toy was sold with a variety of interchangeable parts, or the Dog on Ladder and the Trainer and Leopard are parts from another toy and the base is missing. Whatever the case, this is an ingenious design and an amusing toy.

Attributed to Althof, Bergmann. c. 1870. Tin, pull toy: 7 x 9"; Dog on Ladder: height 9"; Trainer and Leopard: height 6"

Opposite

Front: **Queen in Chariot**

This toy was also produced without the mechanism or figure as a simple chariot pull toy. It appears in the George Brown Sketchbook of 1870 in the same colors.

George W. Brown. 1870. Tin clockwork toy, length 8¼"; height of figure: 5" from bottom of wheel

Rear: **Chariot and Boy Driver**

The toy was also illustrated in the George Brown Sketchbook. The Stevens and Brown catalogue of 1872 described it: "The two-wheel chariot was exuberantly executed and decorated with the circus in mind." The wholesale price was listed as $9 per dozen.

George W. Brown. 1870. Tin, length 18"

Carrousel

This is a delightful out-of-doors wind toy executed by an anonymous craftsman. He was undeniably a person of great imagination, using what materials were immediately available with flair. Four conical metal cups mounted under the base are set to catch the wind and put the carrousel in motion. It is built on a bicycle wheel, mounted on the base of a wooden lamp stand, and turns readily in the slightest wind.

Folk art. Maker unknown; from Philadelphia. c. 1900. Various materials, diameter 24"

Opposite: **Gigantic Circus and Mammoth Hippodrome**

If a toy was a good seller, it usually stayed in the manufacturer's line for years with a few minor changes now and then. This truly great toy, apparently carried for only a few years, possibly had limited sales because of the number of small pieces that made up the toy. The complete circus had to be assembled; when parts were lost it became a frustrating experience.

The painted figures represent clown, bareback rider, trapeze artist, trick mule, and ringmaster. They are all articulated and can be made to do an endless variety of funny things, some anatomically impossible in real life, which adds to the power of the child and thus to the play value of the toy. The whole is set in motion by means of the crank at the left of the photograph. Like other Reed toys the Mammoth Hippodrome when taken apart is packed in a sturdy wooden box.

W. S. Reed. Patented 1880. Wood, box: 15 x 5 x 4"

Above: **Horse with Circus Rider Bell Toy**

The thin wire rockers and the aristocratic lines of the horse give this toy a delicate air. The manufacturer is unidentified. The gymnast's figure closely resembles one shown on a Horse Hoop bell toy in the Althof, Bergmann catalogue of 1874. The horse is brown, the gymnast is dressed in a matching tan and brown combination.

Maker unknown. 1880s. Tin, length 8¼"

Below: **Lion and Elephant Bell Toy**

A yellow lion and a gray elephant are matched, or pitted, in a balancing act. The elephant's blanket, worn down to the basic tin, shows traces of red.

Maker unknown. 1870s. Tin, length 8"; both animals: height 5"

217

THE WORKADAY WORLD

In the years between 1830 and 1900, workaday toys were made for and given to little boys. Being able to control in play the heavy, man's job of loading and emptying a horse-drawn dump truck, the hauling of coal or ice in tin or cast-iron toy trucks complete with chute, shovel, and tongs afforded the nineteenth-century boy feelings of reality and power not often allowed him in his daily transactions.

Transportation toys were among the most popular: they were manageable, working models of the real thing, providing hours of stimulating play.

Fire fighting equipment was equally popular. Volunteer firemen pulled hose reels to fires until the time of the Civil War. As cities grew, paid fire departments were instituted; matched, fast horses became the pride of each fire company. And so...beautifully matched, galloping horses were added to toy fire equipment. If there was a rival it could only have been trains.

From the first snipped-tin, hand-stenciled trains of which so few remain to the first electric models, trains have been played with by father and son, separately and together, later discarded or given away...and then collected.

Steamboat toys came in a poor third. In 1881 a steel steamboat crossed the Atlantic in seven days. Captains gained momentary fame (with crews that worked overtime stoking the fires) cutting hours, then minutes, from previous transatlantic records. News of faster crossings made the

Fire Engine and Firehouse

A most unusual toy, it combines two materials not often used together—the firemen and horses are tin while the rest of the toy is made of wood. The firehouse doors open and close, adding to the play value of the toy; a striker rings a bell inside the firehouse when the door opens, heightening the excitement of seeing the horses and engine respond to an alarm.

Maker unknown. c. 1880. Tin and wood, engine: length 7½"; firehouse: 7 x 12"

219

headlines and boosted the sale of "small, powerful little steamers with hull, boiler, smoke stack and lamp of bright brass that will run about 15 to 20 minutes. $1.25 plus 15 cents postage." Steam provided the most real and exciting element to workaday toys. These toys were particularly attractive to children dedicated to intellectual and scientific pursuits.

All the horse-drawn delivery carts, all the tin and cast-iron horses were well designed and executed; they were readily identified as the counterparts of those seen daily by the Victorian child. What fun to keep the Water Trow, the Ice or Coal Wagon at the door after Mama had dealt with the real delivery man! A child could replicate in play what went on in the world about him—with realistic props.

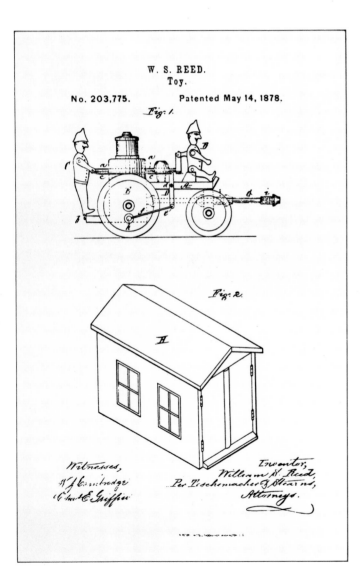

Firehouse and Pumper

In some ways this looks like folk art, but it was in fact a manufactured toy. The firemen are attached to the engine but move forward and backward as the wheels turn. The rod projecting in front of the engine pulls out to a length of 5″ so that the pumper can be pulled to the fire. It was never meant to have horses. When it returns from a fire, it is backed into the wooden fire station. All the excitement of having fire engines with clanging bells made such toys very popular.

W. S. Reed. Patented May 14, 1878. Wood, firehouse: 9 x 10½″; pumper: 8 x 9″

Hook and Ladder

Althof, Bergmann used the pattern stamped in the lantern, so the toy is attributed to them. They did produce a hook and ladder, #506, which closely resembles this one, but is pulled by a horse and has the accompanying driver. An earlier model, this was meant to be pulled by volunteer firemen.

Attributed to Althof, Bergmann. 1875. Tin, length 16"

Left: **Fireman's Hat for Child**

A creditable replica of the real thing—except that it is made of pressed cardboard with a pressed-tin eagle crest—this hat is part of a complete costume package that included an axe, red belt, breastplate, and speaking trumpet. The boy with the speaking trumpet shows the high excitement of the volunteer fireman: the wild rivalry to be first on the scene, to drag the hose reel carriage, to man the pumps, and, particularly, to have the honor of holding the nozzle.

Maker unknown. 1890s. Pressed cardboard and tin, length 12"

Above: **Tin Fire Engines and Firehouse**

Photographed are three good examples of fire engines made in three different sizes by Fallows. The small one on the right is 8" long, the one on the left is 12", and the large one in the rear is 16". All three have orange-red boilers with black tanks. The two larger engines have bells on their undersides with strikers attached to the wheels so that they ring a loud alarm on the way to the fire. All three were made of tin in the 1880s or a little earlier. The firehouse is the same as that on page 218.

223

Opposite: **Hose Reel Carriage**

Although the heart-shaped wheel spokes and the rare heart-shaped embossing on the hose reel are found on wheeled toys attributed to Althof, Bergmann, the overall design in no way resembles their other toys. Gong Bell used just about the same wheel, but they manufactured only bell toys. This hose reel carriage is not included in any known catalogue photographs; the best guess is Althof, Bergmann.

The photograph was taken in front of Carpenters Hall in Philadelphia, which housed one of the first professional societies in the United States.

Althof, Bergmann(?). 1870s. Tin, length 8"

Clockwork Fire Engine with Bell

This is a good replica of the real Lee and Larnard fire engine manufactured in Philadelphia. In the background is a page from the original George Brown Sketchbook, which demonstrates how closely the detail of the design was carried out in the actual toy. The size of the original design in the sketchbook is the same as the manufactured toy.

The front wheels have a pin which can be preset so that the toy goes in a straight line or around in a circle. The fire engine is made of heavy-gauge tin except for the firemen, which are made of white metal. Limited production could account for the fact that so few of this toy have been found.

George W. Brown. Patented 1870. Tin and white metal, length 11", height (to the top of the boiler stack) 7"

Carpenter Fire Engine Company

A complete fire company, this has the four pieces of equipment then in use: a pumper (top), hook and ladder (center), hose cart (bottom row, right), and patrol (bottom row, left). Every cast-iron toy manufacturer put out fire engine sets in several different sizes, ranging from 8″ or 9″ long to this larger-scale set, and even up to 42″. Of all the sets, Carpenter's is probably of the best quality. The pieces were advertised to be "made of malleable iron [which bends—slightly—before breaking], to insure their durability." The *wholesale* price of *each* of the toys was $2.50— then a good week's salary for the workers who made them.

One of the very special features that make the Carpenter toys so attractive is the patented design of wheels attached to the rear legs of the horses, whose long flowing tails give them a realistic impression of galloping when the toy is set in motion, especially those on the Fire Patrol.

Carpenter. Patented November 16, 1880. Cast iron, length: pumper, 18½″; hook and ladder, 26″; patrol, 17″; hose cart, 14″

Overleaf

Left: Atlantic Pumper

Described as "Fire Engine with I. R. hose to throw water," it is shown in the Althof, Bergmann catalogue of 1874 in five different sizes, from 8″ to 15″ long. Several such toys, painted in the traditional fire-engine red, are found in collections; this is the only blue one to have surfaced thus far. The initials I. R. stand for India Rubber. Up to this time, real hoses were made of leather, carefully and most painstakingly stitched by hand so as not to leave any space for the escape of precious fire-arresting water.

Althof, Bergmann. 1874. Tin and cast-iron (wheels), length 9½″

Right: The accompanying steam fire engine, drawn by horses, is also illustrated in the Althof, Bergmann catalogue for 1874, as "#567/2—with two horses, No. 2, Driver and Gong."

Althof, Bergmann. 1874. Tin, length 16″

Opposite: **Steam Fire Engine**

Here is a fire engine complete with valves, cylinders, a balance wheel—"all the essential parts of a modern fire engine," including a whistle. Some people have on occasion referred to this engine as a model, but it was in fact manufactured as a toy. Steam fire engines and boats were not manufactured in such quantities as steam engines alone, which an ingenious child could put to a variety of uses. This, plus their cost ($6.50 retail), possibly explains the fact that so few of the live steam fire engines have been found to date.

This photograph was taken at the famous Head House in the restored Society Hill district of Philadelphia.

Weeden. 1880s. Cast iron and brass, length 18"

Right: A remarkable grouping of rare early American tin toy fire equipment—there are many known examples of cast-iron fire toys but few of tin.

Top: **Hose Reel Carriage**

Fallows. 1880s. Tin, length 17"

Center: **Hook and Ladder**

Fallows. 1880s. Tin, length 21"

Bottom: **Fire Patrol Wagon**

Althof, Bergmann. 1880s. Tin, length 14"

231

"Charles" Hose Reeler

Hose reel carriages, those pulled by volunteer firemen as opposed to later ones drawn by horses and called hose carts, were a popular item with early tin toy manufacturers, most of whom listed several in their catalogues. All quite similar, they differed only in design and size. The "Charles" is the largest size manufactured (the smallest is 6″ long).

The "Charles" has a beautiful sculptured look; the design and execution make it one of the most desirable of the tin fire engine toys.

George W. Brown. c. 1870. Tin with cast-iron wheels, 15 x 23″

Prospect Park Omnibus

The same catalogue illustrates this toy omnibus and the Rail Road Omnibus on the page opposite. They look almost identical, but there are slight differences: in the window design, the seating arrangement for the driver, the shape of the roof, and the vents. The horses on the Prospect Park bus are stationary while the Rail Road horses bob up and down when pulled. This omnibus is just passing in front of the First City Bank in Philadelphia.

Careful scrutiny of these two toys gives us a slant on some shortcuts in manufacturing processes used in the 1870s to keep costs down. The same harness was used for both teams and some parts of both buses, including the wheels, are interchangeable. The horses are operated by different mechanisms but are the same stampings. Yet the Rail Road horses—mounted a bit higher, painted gold, with a contrasting circle around the eye—have a far more dashing aspect. Catching a train was certainly more glamorous in the 1870s, if not more important, than going to the park; the mechanism and the paint convey the message.

Althof, Bergmann. 1874. Tin, length 14"

Opposite: **Rail Road Omnibus**

This jitney is similar to toy #107 in the 1874 Althof, Bergmann catalogue. The fact that the windows in the catalogue line drawing are bell-shaped suggests that the omnibus photographed here is an earlier model, the bell-shaped windows having been introduced later as an "improvement." There is a luggage rack on top for the passengers' convenience.

The photograph was taken in front of an early Pennsylvania spa.

Althof, Bergmann. 1874 or earlier. Tin, length 14"

234

Mass Transportation, Victorian Style

A unique grouping of early tin trolleys, photographed in accurate scale.

Opposite: The topmost cart, 5½″ long, like the 7″ one below (which was made by Merriam), is obviously of early manufacture, possibly also made by Merriam or by any one of the many small Connecticut tin shops. The 10″ Park Trolley below it is of unknown manufacture. The design for the windows of the 11″ Grand Central Depot (marked "G C D") was patented and then assigned to Merriam for manufacture; some collectors attribute this trolley to Althof, Bergmann. The largest, the 15″ City Passengers (bottom), is also of unknown manufacture.

On this page, from top to bottom: the 8″-long trolley is of unknown make; the 9″ trolley is by Fallows; the 14″ Grand Central Depot is of unknown manufacture; the 13″ trolley with conductor was made by Hull and Stafford.

Horse-drawn Trolley

The horse-drawn trolley marked "Worlds Columbian Exposition" is a fine example of the use of lithographed paper on wood. Complete with conductor and driver, it lists the names of all the Chicago streets that were on its route to Jackson Park.

Bliss. 1893. Lithographed paper on wood, length 26"

Opposite: **Locomotive and Tender**

This locomotive and tender were sold together or separately, or with two passenger cars and one U.S. Mail Car, according to 1874 catalogues. Interestingly, these rather unusual windows, used by Althof, Bergmann on trolleys, railroad equipment, boats, carriages, tin banks, and other toys, appear in the drawings for the patent issued to William A. Harwood of Brooklyn in 1873 *(right)*. Harwood was the New York agent for Merriam: was Althof, Bergmann licensed by Merriam or Harwood? Was it piracy or did Merriam manufacture these toys for them? The answers to these questions may never come to light; researchers continue to look and query.

The toys were photographed at the Stratford, Pennsylvania, railroad station.

Althof, Bergmann. c. 1874. Clockwork tin toy, length: locomotive, 12"; coal tender, 5"

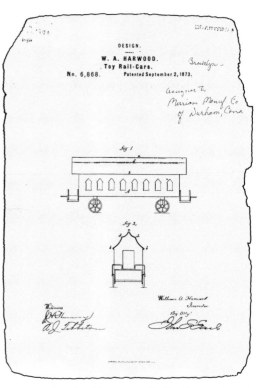

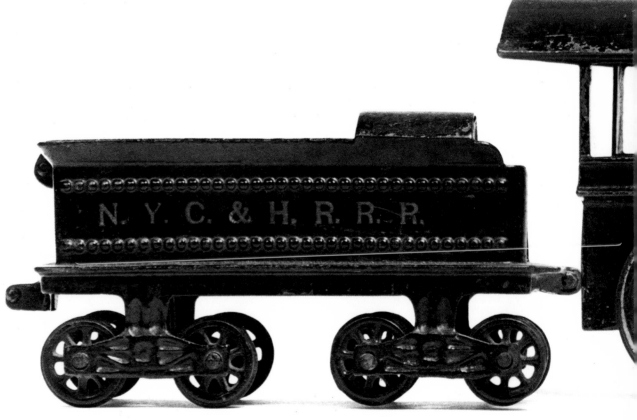

The most unusual feature of "Pegasus" is the tin engineer. His hand is connected to a wire activated by the turning wheels, so that he rings the bell. The locomotive, patented by E. C. Phelps, runs on clock-work springs and gears.

Stevens and Brown. Patented 1874. Tin with cast-iron wheels, 8½ x 12"

Foldout: **999 Buffalo Express**

The largest cast-iron train produced at the time, it appeared in the Pratt and Letchworth 1892 catalogue as "Vestibule Train #FFF." The locomotive boiler is gilt-trimmed black; the wheels are red, as are the stack and domes, the latter also gilt-trimmed. The bell and its frame are of brass; the black cab is trimmed and lettered in gilt; the wheels are red. Both the buffet car and the vestibule coach are olive green. The locomotive was #880.

When the New York to Buffalo express train set a new record of 61.4 miles per hour in 1891, the train was named "The Buffalo Express." Not two years later, the crack New York Central, with the same engineer at the throttle of the engine #999, averaged 112.5 mph, for one measured mile only, so the toy train was renumbered #999.

Pratt and Letchworth. 1893. Cast iron, length 60"

Above: **Clockwork Locomotives**

In the background is an original page from the George Brown Sketchbook (1870), illustrating the U. S. Grant Locomotive and Tender, measuring 15" long. While similar to the Excelsior in the stack, wheels, carriage, and the shape and size of the cab, it appears to have been made as a pull toy; the Excelsior has a clockwork mechanism.

Right: **Excelsior Locomotive**

George W. Brown. 1870. Tin clockwork toy, length 14"

The small train on the far left is the three-wheeled George Brown model, shown on its original box. The small wheel centered on the wooden base is adjustable so that the train can be made to run in a circle.

George W. Brown. 1870. Tin clockwork toy, length 3½"

The red and black train in the middle is very rare. It differs from the George Brown train in the shape of the cab and the smokestack, the arrangement of the wheels, and the design for attaching the bell. Also, it is made of a slightly heavier-gauge tin.

Maker unknown. c. 1870. Tin clockwork toy, length 4"

Left foldout: **Wood Lithographed Boats**

The largest and the smallest lithographed boats to our knowledge—the "Dime Boat," a charming little tugboat, and the "Priscilla," a beautiful example of the use of lithographed printing applied to wood.

The 1896 Christmas catalogue of John M. Smyths Company of Chicago describes the "Priscilla": "It is as near a perfect model of the magnificent boat whose name it bears as it is possible to make a toy. The lithographing is in minute imitation of the Priscilla of the Fall River Line. Equipped with eight life boats, ventilators, sailors, etc.   #445...$1.35."

"Dime Boat"

Maker unknown. 1890s. Lithographed wood, length 6″

"Priscilla"

Bliss. 1890s. Lithographed wood, length 38″

Right foldout: **Wood Lithographed Boats**

Here is a "marina" full of lithographed wood boats from the 1890s, varying in size from 6″ to 38″ long—side-wheelers, paddle-wheelers, ferryboats, a tugboat—by well-known manufacturers.

In the front row, lower right, is the "Providence," probably made by Reed; to its left is an unnamed boat made by Milton Bradley; next is the "Dime Boat"; to its left is the "Columbia," also made by Bradley, which deserves the description from the Montgomery Ward 1894 catalogue:

A perfect reproduction of this powerful and fast war ship, a model of strength and beauty, and the largest and most complete toy cruiser ever made. A feature is the smoke, giving the cruiser the appearance of being under full steam, and moving at a high rate of speed. It is finely lithographed, thoroughly made and rigged with two masts; has four smoke stacks, eight ventilators, wire railing, cord, six boats, cannons etc. and has a crew of twelve officers and sailors. All parts pack inside of boat. 36″ long $0.90.

In the back row, from left to right, are the "Pilgrim" by Reed, and the "Priscilla," the "Gem of the Ocean," and the "Union," all three made by Bliss.

Steamboats

Toy boats were very popular with little boys. City parks built shallow ponds just for boat sailing, and the country offered streams and ponds, so the boats were often sailed in realistic environments. They proved to be so attractive as toys that they were reproduced as indoor pull toys by most of the manufacturers of the day. These are two such toys. The "Crescent" sold at wholesale for $21 per dozen and was also available as a clockwork toy. It is not known if the smaller boat was ever anything but a pull toy.

Right: **"Crescent"**

George W. Brown. 1870. Tin, 6 x 14½"

Left: **Steamboat**

Maker unknown. 1870s. Tin, length 7"

Opposite: **Pleasure Launch**

A collector's dream—an exceptional boat—a pleasure launch made of tin! Most tin boats of the period that have found their way into collections are steamboats, ferryboats, or rigged sailboats. The designer gave this launch, photographed at the Maritime Museum in St. Michaels, Maryland, a very clean, trim look and a style that is timeless.

Fallows. 1880s. Tin, length 13"

Whistler Locomotive and Mechanical Steam Yacht with Whistle

The catalogue description of this locomotive tells us that "whistling locomotives make boys very happy. They have our patented whistling attachment. Very salable. $24.00 per dozen wholesale." It was also made in a 15″ size.

The mechanical steam yachts were available with or without the patented whistle attachment. They also came in two sizes, one 19″ long, the other 23″. With the whistle, the smaller one was $30 per dozen wholesale, and the larger was $48.

Ives. 1880s. Tin clockwork toys, length: locomotive, 12½″; steam yacht, 19″

248

Opposite: **"Flash" Passenger Train**

The locomotive is black with gold lettering, the cab red with gold stenciling on a green base with blue top. The cars too are red, on yellow bases with green tops, also stenciled with a gold stripe. The Lake Shore Railroad was part of the New York Central system. The photograph was taken on a railroad switch in New England.

Fallows. c. 1883. Tin, overall length 33"; cars: each 4½ x 8¼"

Tin and Cast-iron Locomotives

Counterclockwise, from front row, left:

The locomotive pull toy also could be bought with a coal tender and a passenger car with two conductors.

Ives. 1880s. Cast iron, length 7½"

The "Union" locomotive pull toy is easily identified by the yellow cab with painted black windows. It was sold separately or with two passenger cars.

George W. Brown. 1870s. Tin, length 8½"

Educated guessing attributes the "Venus" locomotive to Althof, Bergmann; the painted pattern of the lower part of the base resembles their punched patterns.

Attributed to Althof, Bergmann. 1870s. Tin, length 6"

The large locomotive, sold with cars, was probably manufactured by Hull and Stafford, who often used the combination of a larger wheel with heart-shaped design in back and a plain-spoked wheel in front.

Attributed to Hull and Stafford. 1870s. Tin, length 9¼"

The beautifully made "Victory," typical of Ives products, is designed with a clockwork motor; its front wheels can be turned to move the train in circles of any size.

Ives. 1870s. Tin clockwork toy, length 9"

Opposite above: **Goat Pulling Cart**

One of the larger-scale tin carts, it is driven by a very small man who looks to be about the size of Tom Thumb. The goat is black as pitch, with traces of a bright red on blanket and collar; the little man is dressed in black. The cart is red with gold stenciling and a green interior.

The work cart is typical of those made by Hull and Stafford; in addition to horses they used many different animals to pull small vehicles.

Hull and Stafford. c. 1880. Tin, length 18"

Horse-drawn Milk Cart with Milkman

Several tin toy manufacturers made milk carts, among them Fallows and Althof, Bergmann. It was a popular subject even for later manufacturers of wood, lithographed, and cast-iron toys. This two-wheeled red cart, with the words "PURE MILK" stenciled in gold, is the most realistic in that the two milk cans are removable, adding to the play value and to the stature of the child playing with it. The cans are simply cylindrical tubes with openings in the top which look remarkably as if they were exchangeable with smokestacks for Hull and Stafford trains! The driver, wearing black trousers and hat and a green jacket, is soldered to the seat, which fits on a pin attached to the bottom of the wagon.

Hull and Stafford. 1870s. Tin, length 9½"

Below: **Horse-drawn Cabs**

The toys are attributed to the Merriam Manufacturing Company, but not decisively. Merriam may have made the toy for George Brown, or supplied some of the parts, or vice versa. The cab appears in the George Brown Sketchbook with a slight variation in the window pattern, which may very well have been the difference between the drawing board and the actual production. The arch of the window is identical to that made by Merriam. George Brown made the two sizes shown, Merriam made three, the third being smaller and daintier than either of these.

Both cabs are painted brown with gold stenciling which appears to be the same on both cabs. Once more, whatever their publicity in antique circles today, both Merriam and George Brown started as very small shops; they were located near each other and near the other famous Connecticut tin

257

makers. As research continues it turns out that these families were interrelated by marriage, as if the tin makers were clannish—a kind of closed corporation. We know from bills of sale that they interchanged parts; it now seems that if business was slow or if they were rushed, they farmed out work to each other.

The cab in front is also shown in color *(opposite)* photographed in front of the Philadelphia Academy of Music.

Attributed to Merriam. 1860s. Tin, front cab: 6 x 9"; rear cab: 8 x 13"

Horse-drawn Buckboard

The elegant simplicity of form and design of this toy is unique; it is also the only one known. The original buckboard was a spare vehicle, no springs, with a single board bolted to both axles and a seat fastened to the board. Granted that boards were wide at the time, it was still a minimum means of transport.

The driver is out enjoying the fall foliage in Chadds Ford, Pennsylvania.

Hull and Stafford. 1880s. Tin, length 14"

Above

Left: The same type of delivery wagon was made by several manufacturers.

George W. Brown. 1870. Tin, length 15"

Center: Other companies produced designs similar to this small cab and called them Amish or Delivery Carts.

George W. Brown. 1870s. Tin, length 7½"

Right: Water trows were made by several companies and were popular, for they were a vehicle seen regularly on town and city streets.

George W. Brown. 1870s. Tin, length 7"

Lamppost: see page 264.

Below: **Four-Horse Dray**

The dray was probably made from the molds of the Carpenter two-horse express wagon, with a second team of horses, the cloth top and the post holding it at the four corners added; the body of the wagon and the high driver's seat are identical. This was an excellent use of existing molds to reduce costs.

Carpenter. 1880s. Cast iron, length 24"

Opposite: **Mechanical Horse with Old Lady Driver and Boy Hooking Behind**

The catalogue description calls this a "large, very comical toy" with a "patented galloping horse." The small boy "hooking behind," available in either black or white, provides the novelty and comedy.

Ives. c. 1890. Tin clockwork toy, length 17"

Opposite: **Fancy Goods and Toys Cart**

Fallows was a leader in producing large-sized tin toys. Of course, trains with their many cars were longer, but toy carts 24″ and 26″ long were unusual. In addition to the handsome Fancy Goods and Toys Cart, Fallows produced another toy wagon as a dray, an almost identical wagon, in several editions: "Groceries and Provisions," "Pie Wagon,"

and "U.S. Mail." They cost $10.50 per dozen, wholesale.

Fallows. 1880s. Tin, 11 x 24″

Peddler's Confectionery Wagon

These wagons were made in various sizes; it is believed that this is the largest made by any manufacturer.

Peddlers traveled through the countryside

making regular stops at farmhouses and villages, carrying a wide selection of novelties and household goods, from sewing notions and materials to pots and pans. Housewives who lived in out-of-the-way places looked forward eagerly to the arrival of the peddler's wagon—as did the children, for the peddler always had a box of toys.

Hull and Stafford. c. 1870. Tin, length 23″

Two Horse-drawn Carts and **Lamppost**

Each of these carts gives an excellent idea of its company's patented mechanism to give movement to the horses.

The small horse and cart on the left was made by Carpenter. There is a crank between the two small wheels which lifts the horse's rear legs as the toy rolls forward. They drop by their own weight as the crank turns full circle; this lends a steady cantering motion to the horse. The cart is red with black trim, the horse is white.

Carpenter. 1881. Cast iron, length 10"

The Ives horse on the right has individually attached legs which are coordinated by wires, producing the attractive single-foot gait. The red cart has a blue interior, the black horse has a yellow bridle.

Ives. 1880s. Cast iron, length 9½"

Lamppost

Fallows. 1880s. Tin and glass, height 7¼"

264

Left: "Whips & Cigars" Delivery Cart

An unusual combination of goods—only one other such cart is known, in the collection of the New York Historical Society. The one pictured, red with a black cab and white horses, came with a note enclosed in its box explaining that the toy had belonged to a relative, born July 5, 1853, died June 21, 1858—a not uncommon occurrence as the death rate among children was still high at the time.

Attributed to Merriam. c. 1850. Tin, length 11"

Center: Large Delivery Cart

Fallows made this identical cart, with closed sides and the word "Groceries" painted on it. Some imaginative designer punched out the sides, making an open delivery cart, which gave a new product without the expense of retooling. The body is green with red trim, the roof is blue with gold stenciling, and the horse is brown.

Fallows. 1880s. Tin, length 12"

Right: Small Delivery Cart

When parts were punched from a sheet of tin, the scraps often formed an interesting pattern. Some observant person saw how this particular piece of scrap could be put to good use. Traces of brown paint remain on the cart; the horse is brown.

Attributed to Merriam. c. 1850. Tin, length 9"

Opposite: **Horse-drawn Cart with Barrel**

A well-carved toy—the horse has a sculptural quality and looks more like a show horse than a work horse. It is made of natural wood now weathered to a mellow brown. The toy was photographed in front of a barn built in 1829.

John J. Stoudt, in his *Early Pennsylvania Arts and Crafts* (1964), pictures a very similar horse and cart in figure 190, along with other carved objects. He states:

The set of toys (Fig. #190) probably carved by a young boy reveals a mood almost modern in character with its bold suggestive lines and strong detail. The carved toy was the instrument of childish imagination, the prop for young fantasies, and thus it was destined to show the deep love for animals, generally the common ones around the home. These are characteristic of a tradition which passed when commercial manufacture of toys came.

Folk toy. Illegibly signed on the barrel; probably from Pennsylvania. Dated 1841. Wood, 5 x 9"

Mule and Cart with Driver

This toy, supposedly made by a slave for the child of his master, is an interesting carving, using bits and pieces of materials that were available. The details are quite accurate but the carver obviously had some difficulty with the scale: the driver's hands are greatly out of proportion to the rest of his body; the mule's body is larger than the scale would admit for his head and legs. The black driver is dressed in a white shirt, brown trousers, and a yellow hat with a smart black band.

The photograph was taken in front of an old New England covered bridge with the sign "Reconstructed—1832."

Folk toy. Maker and date unknown. Various materials, length 9"

Butcher Shop

James Edgington of Ross County, Ohio, carved this toy toward the end of the nineteenth century. It was found with a number of his other carvings after his death. They were made for his own amusement and were not sold during his lifetime. Edgington was very imaginative, using what materials he had at hand; an Ohio River fishing boat he carved was made from scraps of a wooden crate originally used to ship Van Houten's cocoa. His artistry is apparent here in the accurate detail of the animals waiting to be sliced into retail cuts.

Folk art. James Edgington. Late 1800s. Wood, 7½ x 10"

269

Combination Lithographed Clockwork Toy

An Ives catalogue from 1893 illustrates all these figures (from left to right): the Butcher, Puss-in-Boots, Spanking Scene, the Carpenter, and the Commercial Traveler. All lithographed on heavy cardboard, they are quite fragile, which undoubtedly accounts for the fact that few remain today.

The figures were sold separately and together in a package as both "Toy Steam Engine attachments each having a pulley and cord" and "Hot Air Toys for Stove Pipes or Radiators," which could be operated wher-

ever there was a current of air. But this toy has a clockwork mechanism. It is still in its original box with the factory number, 355. The printed label reads, "One piece—clockwork, combination—I. B. & Co." When wound the butcher chops meat, the dog pulls the cat's tail, the boy gets spanked, the man saws wood, and the commercial traveler doffs his hat.

Ives. c. 1893. Lithographed paper on wood, overall length 29"; figures: from 4" to 7" long and from 3" to 6" high

Opposite: **"The Old Nurse"**

The nurse rocks forward and back in a very
natural movement as she tosses her little
white charge up in the air. The movement is
regulated by a clockwork spring. It was described in the manufacturer's 1893 catalogue
as "a very comical mechanical toy."

Ives. c. 1875. Tin, height 9½"

Mason Bank #9

A coin is placed in the hod, the lever is pressed, and the hod goes
forward, depositing the coin. At the same time the bricklayer
raises his hand and places the brick in position as he raises and
lowers his trowel.

J. and E. Stevens. Patented February 8, 1887. Cast iron, 7 x 7½"

Front: **Washerwoman Bell Toy**

As the bell toy is pulled the washerwoman moves forward and back
and her hands go up and down, seeming to wash the clothes—a
cloth attached to her hands. The same tin face nailed to the round
wooden head and neck was available in either black or white. The
figure of the woman is the same as that used on many Ives toys.

Attributed to Ives. 1880s. Cast iron, length 8"

Rear: **Washerwoman**

The clockwork washerwoman moves up and down. She too has
cloth attached to her hands, so that as she moves the clothes get
scrubbed on the washboard.

Attributed to Ives. 1880s. Clockwork toy on a wood base, 5 x 10"

Wood Sawyer

The old leather washers identify this wind toy as an early carving. Found in the Lancaster, Pennsylvania area, it is attributed to an unknown Pennsylvania craftsman.

When a current of air catches in the tin blades they turn, setting the sawyer to sawing his log. Probably made in the last quarter of the nineteenth century, the sawyer seems to have been fashioned after the hot-air toys produced commercially by Ives.

Folk art. Maker unknown; from Pennsylvania. Late 1800s. Wood and tin, 12 x 8"

Man Chopping Wood

At first glance this looks like a piece of folk art, but it is a manufactured toy. The woodcutter has a composition head and a metal hat. Like other Ives figures he has cast-metal legs and hands and a wooden body, here clothed in a blue jacket and gray trousers.

As the clockwork unwinds the man lowers his axe to chop the log, displaying the same type of bending action as that in the Suffragette (see page 73) and other Ives automatons.

Ives. 1890s. Various materials, height 10½"

Boy Sawing Wood

The blue-japanned boy is mounted on a dark green oval treadle on a bright red tin base. As the toy is pulled, a concentric wheel activates the boy so that he saws the wooden log—a never-ending task!

There exists a similar toy, with the same figure on the same base and the same simple mechanism, but that boy is chopping wood. They are obviously made by the same company.

Attributed to Althof, Bergmann. 1875–80. Tin, 3½ x 6¼"

IDENTIFICATION AND TRADEMARKS

Tower Sand Toy

Without any doubt this is one of the earliest wooden playthings commercially produced in the United States. Very few Tower Guild toys are known. The Sand Toy is identical to one in the Margaret Strong Museum in Rochester, New York, which still bears the label, "Manufactured by the William S. Tower Company, South Hingham, Mass. Patent applied for." The main features and the clothing pattern are thinly painted or printed black lines.

Sand is poured into the box, trickles down through a small opening, and falls on the paddles of the wheel, setting it in motion, which in turn sets the surprised-looking country boy to cranking the wheel. The box originally had a sliding lid.

Below is the original trade sign which hung in front of the Tower factory. It is black with gold lettering and measures 9½ x 36".

William S. Tower. 1830s. Wood, 9 x 11 x 5"

Patent dates were cast into the base or coin trap of many mechanical banks which are often traceable through the patent papers. Occasionally we find a company name (Stevens) or location (Buffalo, New York) with the patent date.

In the early days (the 1700s), craftsmen put something of themselves into their toys, which they made mainly for children they knew or for children within a small radius of their homes. Only the peddlers traveled distances—or fathers who went to Boston, New York, or Philadelphia for politics or on business and who might bring home a toy from one of the novelty shops in those cities. All these toys predate advertising campaigns. Charles M. Crandall, who placed large, illustrated advertisements in the *American Agriculturist*, which had a wide retail circulation, was an exception. City directory ads were meant for the trade, not for the retail market.

As an example of problems in the identification of toys: from 1868 to 1873, one R. J. Clay patented and made several "mechanical toys" under the company name of Automatic Toy Works. By 1874 his patents were assigned to E. R. Ives. In a copiously illustrated 1893 catalogue, the Ives, Blakeslee and Williams Company announced a line of "new and original mechanical toys." It is nowhere mentioned that these are Clay patents, or that they had been designed, produced, and marketed by the Automatic Toy Works twenty to twenty-five years earlier!

In the same catalogue, many toys have been positively identified as products of other manufacturers. It is as if a number of toy manufacturers had disappeared in the great depression that climaxed in 1893, and that Ives, Blakeslee and Williams, who had been associated with

one another at various times over the previous three decades, had pooled their resources, bought up all available inventories, and listed them in this catalogue. Business and census records show that in the late 1860s and early 1870s many small businesses, including toy companies, sprang up almost overnight and closed almost as quickly, which adds to the confusion of identifying manufacturers.

Thus, identification of a toy exclusively by catalogue, unless it be the manufacturer's dated catalogue illustrating the specific toy—not a similar toy; not in a jobber's catalogue; not an approximate date—cannot be positive. Even with a dated catalogue, where there is no history of the manufacturer, where no business records can be found, identification can still be a matter of doubt, for there is no way of know-

ing whether or not the company manufactured or simply assembled and decorated the toy, whether they acquired designs or inventories from defunct companies, or whether they imported parts or even the whole toy. The latter is less likely, for continuing research shows that newspaper ads, city directories, and mail-order houses usually listed the imported toys separately.

For knowledgeable collectors this poses no serious problem. Whether assembled, taken over, manufactured in a shop in the toy maker's backyard or in a city factory, the *toy* is the thing. The design, condition, approximate date, history—if there is a documented story attached—these are the valuable ingredients. For the collector who is into toys solely for investment purposes, documentation, rarity, and resale value are undoubtedly the most important factors. A caution: there are those who like to see a buyer happy and who will make up a believable background on a toy to please a customer. Also, over the years memories fade and details may well become dim or confused as stories are handed down. Caveat emptor.

Bliss used the trademark of an anchor with the initial B in the center and the name Bliss within a heart-shaped design.

George W. Brown pasted a printed label on the box the toy was packed in, which sometimes formed an integral part of the toy.

Buffalo Toys (also known as **Pratt and Letchworth**) sometimes used a picture of a buffalo as a trademark in its catalogue.

Almost every **Charles M. Crandall** toy seen in its original box has the name and patent date printed on the sturdy wooden box, many of which have survived.

James Fallows and Company used the Roman numerals IXL on many of its toys. Interpreted as "I excel," it also may denote the date of his arrival in the United States and the date of his first tin toy.

Francis, Field and Francis, when it identified its toys, used a plate embossed with the company name or stamped the name on the bottom of the toy.

One **Ives** toy in the collection, the hansom cab with rubber tires, had a metal nameplate affixed: The Ives Manufacturing Corporation. Some of its toys are recognizable by the patent date that was part of the mold, usually found on the shaft of horse-drawn toys. This was true of the **Carpenter** toys as well. The latter company sometimes marked its toys under the seat of the cart or wagon. Carpenter also sometimes used the mark XL.

Kenton Hardware used the trademark Kentontoys.

The **W. S. Reed Company** name, and usually the patent date, was clearly printed on the box, also often an integral part of the toy, or on a label.

Tower Toy Guild toys and doll furniture were identified with small gummed paper labels, few of which have survived. Specific pieces were labeled with the name of the individual craftsman: Loring Cushing, Samuel Hersey, etc.

THE MANUFACTURERS

Early manufacturers prided themselves on the quality of their work and their products; however, errors *did* sometimes slip by. As in many fields of collecting, a production error increases the desirability and value of the toy.

The stenciler applying the screen to the George Brown Excelsior Locomotive did it right on one side, but when he turned the locomotive around he did the other side backwards!

The tin wagon marked "Express" has the *s*'s in reverse.

Althof, Bergmann and Co.
Bergmann Brothers were New York City jobbers, c. 1860. In 1867 they joined forces with L. Althof, continuing as jobbers until 1874, when Althof, together with another man, procured two toy patents. They then commissioned toys and may have manufactured/assembled some of their own. Tin toys and tin still banks.

American Toy Company
Not a manufacturer, but New York City wholesale showroom and sales representatives for George W. Brown and the merged Stevens and Brown companies from 1868 to 1872. Cast-iron and tin toys.

Art Fabric Mills
New Haven, Connecticut, 1890s. Printed cloth for stuffed dolls and tenpins.

Automatic Toy Works
Founded by designer and inventor R. J. Clay in 1868; his line of mechanical windup toys was bought out by Ives in 1874. Clay continued to make blocks and toy watches into the 1880s, under his own name.

R. Bliss Mfg. Co.
Founded in Providence, Rhode Island, in 1832, later moved to Pawtucket where it continued until the 1890s, manufacturing tool chests (real as well as toy), parlor games, hardwood and lithographed blocks, and toys. It is best known for dollhouses, boats, and trains.

Milton Bradley Company
Springfield, Massachusetts, 1860–present. A progressive, concerned firm, it made games and a wide variety of toys. Today, it is still one of the biggest and best suppliers of educational materials.

George W. Brown and Company
Founded 1856, Forestville, Connecticut. (There is some evidence that George Brown made tin toys as early as 1850 while still a clockmaker, or even a clockmaker's apprentice.) Merged with J. and E. Stevens in 1868; firm dissolved in 1880. Tin and clockwork toys.

Buffalo Toy Works
See Pratt and Letchworth

C. C. Bush and Company
Providence, Rhode Island, c. 1870. Kaleidoscopes and other optical toys.

Francis W. Carpenter and Company
Harrison, New York, 1894–1925. Cast-iron and malleable-iron toys.

Charles M. Crandall Company
Founded by Charles's father, Asa, Covington, Pennsylvania, c. 1820; Montrose, Pennsylvania, 1866; Waverly, New York, 1885 (renamed Waverly Toy Works, with Moses Lyman, attorney); company closed after Crandall's death in 1905. Wood toys, games.

Jesse Crandall
Brooklyn, New York, 1840s–80s. Crandall was involved in the invention, design, manufacture, and sale, both wholesale and retail, of toys, particularly of hobby, rocking, and shoofly horses, velocipedes, and games.

James Fallows and Son
Philadelphia, Pennsylvania. On January 1, 1870, it was organized as "C. B. Porter and Company, Manufacturers of Japanned, Pressed and Plain Tinware etc.," with *no* mention of toys. This firm was a continuation of Francis, Field and Francis (*see* below). Although James Fallows was the designer/inventor and "superintended the practical operations of the factory" (so that the toys produced had been and were, in fact, Fallows toys), the firm did not carry his name until about 1880. Tin toys.

Francis, Field and Francis
Philadelphia, Pennsylvania. A direct continuation of Henry and Thomas Francis, 1830s; became Francis, Field and Francis c. 1838; changed hands several times before 1870, when James Fallows became involved with the company (*see* above). Japanned tin toys and housewares; also importers. (*See* Philadelphia Tin Toy)

Gibbs Manufacturing Company
Canton, Ohio, c. 1890–present. Pull and push toys, tops, and other toys.

E. Perry Gleason
Providence, Rhode Island, 1880s. Bagatelle games.

Gong Bell Mfg. Co.
East Hampton, Connecticut; 1866–late 1930s. Hardware bells and bell toys.

A. D. Handy
Boston, Massachusetts, 1880s–90s. Stereopticon supplies.

N. N. Hill Brass Co.
East Hampton, Connecticut, 1889–1930s. Branch of the National Novelty Corporation, New York. Manufacturers of bells and bell toys.

S. L. Hill
New York, New York, c. 1858–80s. Blocks, boxes.

The Hubley Manufacturing Co.
Lancaster, Pennsylvania, 1894–1940s. Cast-iron toys, banks, cap guns.

Hull and Stafford
Established as Hull and Wright, c. 1860. Clinton, Connecticut, 1866–80s. Acquired Union Manufacturing Company in 1869. Tin toys.

E. R. Ives and Company
Established in 1868 in Plymouth, Connecticut. In early 1870s was joined by C. Blakeslee and the firm became known as Ives and Blakeslee Company. Moved from Plymouth to Bridgeport, Connecticut. Acquired Jerome Secor, then R. J. Clary, c. 1874. In the early 1890s the firm was known as Ives, Blakeslee and Williams Company (jobbers as well as manufacturers). Failed in 1929. Cast-iron, tin, and clockwork toys.

Kenton Hardware Company
Kenton, Ohio, 1880s. Cast-iron toys and banks.

Kyser and Rex
Philadelphia, Pennsylvania, 1880–84. Patented cast-iron toys and mechanical banks. From 1884 to 1890, Alfred Rex continued to patent mechanical banks and licensed them to other manufacturers.

McLoughlin Brothers
New York, New York, 1854–1921 (the 1828 date sometimes given is that of an unknown company which the McLoughlin Brothers took over in 1854). Picture books, paper dolls, dollhouses, games, optical toys, and children's books.

Merriam Manufacturing Company
Durham, Connecticut, 1856–present (the company ceased making toys in the 1880s; currently manufactures boxes). Tin toys and household goods.

The Metropolitan Syndicate Press
Chicago, Illinois, c. 1900. Stereoscopic views.

National Toy Company
New York, New York, 1870s. Wholesale distributors to the toy trade; general toys.

Parker Brothers, Inc.
Salem, Massachusetts, 1883–present. Board games, puzzles, children's books.

Philadelphia Tin Toy
This name appeared in Philadelphia advertisements from 1847 into the 1850s for the toy line made by Francis, Field and Francis.

Pratt and Letchworth
Buffalo, New York, 1880–90s. Marketed toys under the name Buffalo Toy Works as well; also called the Buffalo Indestructible Malleable Iron and Steel Toy Works. Iron and steel toys.

W. S. Reed Toy Company
Leominster, Massachusetts, 1875–97. Taken over and renamed the Whitney Reed Chair Company in 1898. Wood toys.

C. G. Shepard and Company
Buffalo, New York, 1866. Tin horns, still and mechanical banks.

William Shimer Son and Co.
Freemansburg, Pennsylvania, 1875–80s. Cast-iron toys, mechanical banks.

J. and E. Stevens and Company
Cromwell, Connecticut, 1843–c. 1930. Hardware, cast-iron toys, mechanical banks, toy guns and pistols. (*See* American Toy Company, 1868–72; Stevens and Brown, 1868–72.)

The Stevens and Brown Manufacturing Co.
Resulted from the merger of George W. Brown and Company and J. and E. Stevens and Company in late 1868. The partnership lasted until 1872.

William S. Tower
South Hingham, Massachusetts, 1830s–c. 1880. Known also as Tower Toy Guild; Tower Toy Company; W. S. Tower Toy Company. Wood toys, doll furniture.

Union Manufacturing Company
Clinton, Connecticut, 1853–69. Acquired by Hull and Stafford in 1869. Tin toys.

United States Hardware Company
New Haven, Connecticut, 1896–1901. Cast-iron toys and Fairy Rubber Balls.

Watrous Manufacturing Co.
East Hampton, Connecticut; 1880s–1930s. Merged with N. N. Hill, c. 1890; branch of the National Novelty Corporation, New York. Rattles, reins, bells of all kinds, bell toys.

Weeden Manufacturing Co.
New Bedford, Massachusetts, 1880s. Steam engines and toys.

Welker and Crosby
Brooklyn, New York, 1885–88. Cast-iron horse-drawn vehicles. (Crosby was later employed by Pratt and Letchworth.)

Wilkins Toy Works
Keene, New Hampshire, 1888. Went from making washing machine wringers to toy wringers. Cast-iron and steel toys. Acquired by Kingsbury Manufacturing Company in 1894 (currently tool and die makers).

BIBLIOGRAPHY

Belcher, Joseph. *Two Sermons Preached in Dedham*. Boston, 1710.

Brown, George W. *The George Brown Toy Sketchbook*. Edited and introduced by Edith Barenholtz. Princeton, N.J., 1971.

Calhoun, Arthur W. *A Social History of the American Family*. Cleveland, 1917.

Carnegie, Andrew. *The Gospel of Wealth, and Other Timely Essays*. Edited by Edward C. Kirkland. Cambridge, Mass., 1962.

Cotton, John. *A Practical Commentary*. London, 1656.

Coxe, Tenche. *View of the United States of America*. Philadelphia, 1794.

Cremin, Lawrence A. *American Education: The Colonial Experience 1607–1783*. New York, 1970.

D'Allemagne, Henri. *Histoire des Jouets*. Paris, 1927.

Davidson, Marshall. *Life in America*. 2 vols. Boston, 1951.

Dickens, Charles. *American Notes*. London, 1842.

Earle, Alice Morse. *Child Life in Colonial Days*. New York, 1899.

Fleming, Sandford. *Children and Puritanism*. New Haven, Conn., 1933.

Greven, Philip J. *The Protestant Temperament*. New York, 1977.

Hertz, Louis. *Handbook of Old American Toys*. Wethersfield, Conn., 1947.

————. *The Toy Collector*. New York, 1969.

Hillier, Mary. *Automata and Mechanical Toys*. London, 1976.

Hoar, G. F. *Autobiography of Seventy Years*. New York, 1903.

Hoyle's Games. London, 1796.

Little Charley's Games and Sports. Philadelphia, 1852.

McClintock, Marshall and Inez. *Toys in America*. Washington, D.C., 1961.

McClinton, Katharine. *Antiques of American Childhood*. New York, 1970.

Martineau, Harriet. *Society in America*. New York, 1837.

Meyer, John. *A Handbook of Old Mechanical Penny Banks*. 1952. Reissued as *Old Penny Banks*, with Larry Freeman. Watkins Glen, N.Y., 1960.

Morgan, Edmund S. *The Puritan Family*. New York, 1944.

Morgan, H. W., ed. *The Gilded Age: An Age in Need of Reinterpretation*. Syracuse, N.Y., 1963.

Parrington, Vernon L. *Main Currents in American Thought*. 3 vols. New York, 1927–30.

Pressland, David. *The Art of the Tin Toy*. New York, 1976.

Remise, Jac, and Fondin, Jean. *The Golden Age of Toys*. Greenwich, Conn., 1967.

Stoudt, John J. *Early Pennsylvania Arts and Crafts*. New York, 1964.

Thomas, Isaiah. *A Little Pretty Pocket Book*. Worcester, Mass., 1787.

Wadsworth, Benjamin. *The Well-Ordered Family*. Boston, 1712.

Warner, Jr., S. B. *Streetcar Suburbs: The Process of Growth in Boston 1870–1900*. Cambridge, Mass., 1962.

Wilder, Laura Ingalls. The *Little House* Series. New York, 1940s–50s.

Winthrop, John. *The History of New England from 1630 to 1649*. Boston, 1825–26.

Periodicals and Other Sources

American Agriculturist
Godey's Lady's Book
Harper's Bazar
St. Nicholas
Youth's Companion
City directories
Montgomery Ward catalogues, 1877–1900
Oscar Strassburger & Co. Catalogue, 1880
Old catalogues and reprint editions of the following toy companies:

Althof, Bergmann and Co.; R. Bliss Mfg. Co.; Buffalo Toy Works; Francis W. Carpenter and Company; N. N. Hill Brass Co.; Hubley Manufacturing Co.; Hull and Stafford; Ives, Blakeslee and Williams Company; Kenton Hardware Company; Merriam Manufacturing Company; McLoughlin Brothers; National Toy Company; William Shimer Son and Co.; Stevens and Brown Manufacturing Co.; United States Hardware Company; Watrous Manufacturing Co.; Whitney Reed Chair Co.; Wilkins Toy Works

INDEX TO THE PLATES

All numbers refer to pages on which the plates appear

CREDITS

Grateful acknowledgment is made for permission to quote from the following works:

Antiques of American Childhood by Katharine Morrison McClinton, Copyright © 1970 by Katharine Morrison McClinton; used by permission of Bramhall House, a division of Clarkson N. Potter, Inc. "Pilgrims and Puritans" from *A Book of Americans* by Rosemary and Stephen Vincent Benét, Copyright 1933 by Rosemary and Stephen Vincent Benét; Copyright renewed © by Rosemary Carr Benét; reprinted by permission of Brandt & Brandt Literary Agents, Inc. *Books, Children and Men* by Paul Hazard, The Horn Book, Inc. *Early Pennsylvania Arts and Crafts* by J. J. Stoudt, by permission of the publisher, © A. S. Barnes & Co., all rights reserved. *Main Currents in American Thought* by Vernon Parrington, Harcourt Brace Jovanovich, Inc. *Old Mechanical Penny Banks*, plus new material from *Still Banks*, by John D. Meyers, with additions by G. L. Freeman, Century House Publishing, Inc., Watkins Glen, N.Y.